Be Happy Now

Claim the Life You Deserve

By
Katie B. Smith

Copyright © 2018 by Katie B. Smith

All rights reserved.

No part of this book may be reproduced in any form or by any electronic or mechanical means including information storage and retrieval systems, without permission in writing from the author. The only exception is by a reviewer, who may quote short excerpts in a review.

Paperback ISBN: 978-1-62747-121-3
eBook ISBN: 978-1-62747-115-2

Book design by Choice Digital Marketing Agency

Front Cover Image: © | 2017 Katie B. Smith

Back Cover Image: © | 2017 Katie B. Smith

Written by Katie B. Smith

Visit my website at www.katiebsmith.com

Printed in the United States of America

First Printing: November 2017

Published by: Sojourn Publishing, LLC

Published for: Katie B. Smith & Associates, LLC

TABLE OF CONTENTS

INTRODUCTION v

ACKNOWLEDGMENTS ix

INTRODUCTION TO MAGIC xi

Chapter 1: Body Wisdom 1

    Fear 1
    Breath 6
    Reinvention 13
    Resistance 15
    Grace 21

Chapter 2: Mindful Matters 23

    Masculine & Feminine 23
    Self-Observation 26
    Guilt 31
    Everything as Your Teacher 32
    Relationships as Mirrors 34
    Myth Busting 42
    Tolerations versus Acceptance 48

Chapter 3: Awakening Your Heart 55

    Courage 55
    Forgiveness 58

Death, Rebirth and Reclamation 61
Commitment 65
Acknowledgment – The Love Balm 74
Leaving a Legacy 78
Choices 82
Rituals, Intention and Living with Reverence 86

Chapter 4: My Life as a Gift 89

Being Alive in Life 92
Quotations to Empower 95
Clients' Thoughts 103

BIBLIOGRAPHY 113

INTRODUCTION

Who are you? Really?

You are the sun glistening on the ocean, the mist in the trees – you are so much more than you can imagine or realize. You are the breath of GOD, you are the eyes of the world, you are the touch of softness and love. I am so amazed at all we embody and all we behold. How is it that we forget, and get caught in the distractions of our lives, in the negative pettiness we engage in every day? How is it we forget who we are when our essence is so magnificent, so strong, and so clear?

We so easily let our attention wander, losing sight of our spirit. We ignore it, letting the outside world influence our focus with its comparisons and judgments. So how do we start to live infused and integrated with spirit? How do we shift our thinking and truly be in the space of love?

Making these changes will require baby steps, attention, and presence in all parts of your life – your work, your relationships, your parenting – and a commitment to looking at how you choose to lead yourself in this life. The key is awareness. Awareness will help bring you fully into your life. It will help you speak, observe, and interact while remaining true to yourself. Awareness is powerful. This book is about how to awaken it in your work and your life to create a happy, fulfilled experience while you are here.

You start by just noticing where you are at any given time and observe it without judgment. By looking at and putting attention on yourself, instead of everyone else. Actually, it is everyone else who can help you notice yourself.

Whatever you see in others is a clue to what is happening within you. Let others become your mirror, and take that reflection back into yourself. This is what Margi held for me, the reflection of what I aspired to. Marji was a dear friend, mentor and yoga student of mine. I kept taking her reflection back into me and knowing that someday I would recognize it in myself. It takes time, and it is important to sit in silence with yourself. It takes time to listen to your heart instead of your head, to notice how your body feels, and to listen to what your still, small voice is saying. By doing this, you can begin to trust your heart. By creating space for this time, and then putting a new belief and behavior in place, you create a different brain pattern.

You will begin to shift your perspective from outward to inward, from external to internal, into the sacred chamber of the heart. For who you really are resides there, and it just needs attention to allow your voice to be heard. Awareness is what allows you to see your choices for what they really are. It shapes how you live and experience your life. Awareness is how you "be" in the world. If you don't allow awareness in your heart, how can you expect to express more love, more gentleness with yourself? If you don't give this attention to yourself, how can you expect to give that attention to others? Your positive attention, your gentleness, is about acting from the space of love, not obligation. It is created out of internal desire, not out of external pressure or expectation. It becomes a way of being that you desire to experience, versus a task marked off your "to-do" list.

You feel and know this desire intrinsically. See, this is what you are made of, and you have just forgotten it. It isn't as hard as you think, because you do not have to create something new. You are simply remembering who you really are. This is made easier by relaxing into yourself, and allowing your heart to soften, open, feel and heal. If you don't incorporate your body and your feelings, you can't expand your awareness. The integration of both the body and heart is an important part in expanding this knowledge of awareness. It is also key in helping you remember that what you are is what you feel in your heart.

Close your eyes and breathe deeply. Observe what you are feeling. What do you feel when you allow yourself to sink into your body and your heart? Imagine your body as a battery, only made up of energy. Some parts have more energy than others, more charge or voltage. What is the quality of the energy you feel? Take a moment to close your eyes and let this question sink in. What is your body wisdom telling you? We will learn how to begin to listen to your body wisdom in this book, and take notice of what it is telling you.

Your body is so wise, and sometimes we tend to ignore it and abuse it and treat it like it doesn't matter. The body houses your magnificent heart and soul; it houses your creative genius, your intelligence, your peace, your love and your fear. The body manages all the stress you put on it – and look at how amazing you are. When was the last time you paid homage to your body? When was the last time you honored what is in your heart? When was the last time you sat with your pain and the parts of your body that were stressed?

I didn't have a lot of money when my kids were young, so on Friday nights we would have dinner. Then I would give the kids baths, and afterward, we would go into our yoga room that looked out at the Pacific Ocean. We would dance and have massage time.

At the time, I dabbled in learning about acupressure points and massage and practiced every Friday night on my kids until they drifted off to sleep in a relaxed state. To this day, they both live fully in their bodies, love touch and gentleness, and are tuned in to their intuition. At the time, I was living in Half Moon Bay,

California, and it was such a special time in my growth and development, and in the kids' lives. I was being taught to tap into my internal strength emotionally, and my capacity to love. I learned how to receive support and ask for support.

I look back now and see that I didn't even realize how beautiful I was, not outwardly but inwardly. I was so confronted with my negative mind and my inability to make enough money. I was always worrying so much about my kids and the unknown territory of life as a single mom, that I couldn't see the magic right in front of me. Now, twenty years later, I look back and realize how beautiful I am (from the inside out) and how powerful a life can be. I realize how much my awareness has grown, and how much I have learned that loving myself is key to creating more happiness in my life.

I write this book in honor of my commitment to growth for you as well as for myself. Through it I consider the next phase of my growth into my potential by sharing my voice and perspective and what helped me navigate the unknown territory of falling in love with myself. Once we do this, we have even more love to share with others. My prayer is that in some way this book will support you in doing the same with your life in whatever way that works for you, and together our love can make a positive impact in our world.

May this book offer you a template to view and love your own life in your own unique, magical way, and to learn to no longer live in "silos" (separate compartments, where you're someone different at work than at home) but to live integrated in who you are wherever you are. To be able to lead yourself from your vulnerable, authentic and magnificent nature, no matter if you are a professional or a householder. May you be liberated in your ability to show who you really are to the world.

All the names in this book have been changed to protect the identity of the individuals.

ACKNOWLEDGMENTS

Margi Miller was my reflection of the love inside of me. She was the constant reminder that living from love is possible – and I just needed to put attention on what I wanted to create in my life and in myself, in order to harness and experience a life of love and inspiration the way she loved and inspired.

I am so grateful Margi came into my life and became such a powerful friend and mentor. I will hold her in my heart forever. She knew how to hold magic – always happy, always smiling, even when things were not going well. The last time we met she had been diagnosed with cancer and was getting treated and she was still so happy, living in a positive frame of mind, even in the midst of cancer. She was always a reflection for me of how not to fall into the grips of my "victim" thinking and how not to let it take over who I was.

Her presence lives in me even though her body is not here. I think it is interesting that we both went into coaching and took two different paths – and who would have thought she would end up with pancreatic cancer and die so young. She was such a beautiful soul. I do think that when we are done, we are done. By that I mean that Margi completed her assignment here. She transitioned to help probably thousands of other people like me loving from the "other side."

She knew how to reflect encouragement, honor, and integrity, and always praised the essence of who I was. She communicated that to me from the first day she walked into my Kundalini Yoga class, when I was teaching at the Montara

Lighthouse in Half Moon Bay, California. I was so blown away by the experience she had and her recognition of the power of this yogic technology. Margi always saw me for who I was, even when I did not see my own vibrant light. As I write this book, she comes to me and tells me to write about living an authentic life, an integrated life. To show the tools I have used and integrated in my own career, in business, with my kids and in my personal life.

As for the struggles, the victories, the commitment to growth and my own awareness, she always commented to me about my level of commitment to living true to who I am. This book is in honor of her, believing in me when I did not believe in myself. She communicated to me how strong I was, and praised the depth of my love and beauty and commitment to living a conscious path. In the midst of my struggle, she continually reflected my true nature back to me. I will be forever grateful for her friendship, her love and her time here on earth.

All those who knew her were left a better person because of her presence. This is the example of the legacy I want to leave. I want to leave everyone I engaged with a better person, because of our interaction.

INTRODUCTION TO MAGIC

Magic – "Those who don't believe in magic will never find it." – Roald Dahl

I have heard magic described as a magnificent amount of grace and invisible commitment. My first realization of the possibility of living in a state of magic came to me when I was living in Half Moon Bay (HMB), California. I was teaching yoga part-time and doing recruiting for big-box retailers. I had just gotten into the recruiting business with a one-woman shop on the coast and she was willing to work around my kids' schedules and my yoga schedules, so it worked out. Plus, she paid for insurance, which was a big deal, considering I had a daughter, Renee, who had a cochlear implant and needed insurance to cover regular visits to the audiologists. I was making $35K annually, in 1995, and I was trying to support two kids on this income. I had left my husband because he was an alcoholic, and he was struggling with emotional abuse from his father. He was occupied on his own journey of healing, and was not able to be available for us.

We were evicted from our home, because we hadn't paid rent and I realized I needed to leave. I was lying on the chiropractic table and Margi Miller was lying beside me. Margi was one of my devoted yoga students, in her mid-forties, and she was a single mom herself. The chiropractor adjusted me, and I just started sobbing. I knew I was going to move out and had started packing the house, but had no clue where I would get the money to move or where I would go. Margi asked me what was going on, as she knew my situation with my marriage.

I told her I realized I could no longer stay in my marriage, and I was trying to not let money be a factor, but wasn't sure where or how it was all going to happen. I continued sobbing and Margi slipped a check under my table for $1400.00. She said, "This will cover my yoga classes for the next year." Then she came up to me and said, "You come to my house with the kids and you can stay there until you figure out your next move."

Magic: it happens when you least expect it. My prayers had been answered. I had a place to go and money to hire the movers. From there, I was not sure what would happen, but I had a next step.

I moved out one morning after John (my husband) had come home the night before, stone drunk and angry. I was scared, he slept on the futon in the front room, and at 2 AM I slipped out to my friend's house, fearing he would fight with me, which would wake up the kids. Amy, my friend, had given me a key to her house the day before, saying that if John gets violent or I get scared, that I should come to her house with the kids. I woke up at 5 AM, went back to my house, and got the kids up, dressed, and fed, while John was passed out on the futon. It was a school day that day, and I was relieved that the kids both had overnight places to stay the next night while I moved our things out.

Meg, my sister who lived in San Francisco, had met me at 6AM to go with me to drop off the kids. I lived in a small bedroom community on the California coast. I had reflections of healthy families all around me – and that was all I wanted. But the Divine had other plans for me. We were being transformed and didn't know it, both John and I. The kids were off, and then the moving truck came. John got up and showered, and took off for work. He was so angry at me, but never said a word. I was grateful my sister was there and I was not alone.

John never physically harmed me or the kids, but when he drank, the alcohol took over with words and emotions. For a week, I had been packing boxes and he was asking why I was packing – and I said, "We are being evicted. I am moving out." He was in deep denial of the reality of our situation. He never thought I would really do it, I guess.

Meg and several wonderful yoga students showed up after John left and helped me with the movers. I remember sitting in the living room crying, sobbing so hard at this ending, this death to a part of myself and the life I had dreamed of. I remember sitting in the tension of this new beginning and not knowing where I would go or what would come next. I was sobbing in fear of the unknown, having made the choice to dive straight into my fear. My neighbors came over, two older brothers in their eighties. They had seen the moving truck and asked my sister what was going on. When she told them, they came over and handed me two hundred-dollar bills. That made me sob even more, as I was so touched by their gesture, their concern for me and the kids. It was amazing to have received this gift from them.

On top of all that, my yoga students had come to support and serve me in moving and loading the truck. I was overwhelmed with emotion and the support that surrounded me. I left a lot of stuff at the house, but I took what I thought was most important and we hauled it to a storage unit.

When I think of my kids, I can't imagine what was going through their heads, wondering why their world had been turned upside down. I am sure I explained to them what was happening, but at that age, how does any child understand? My son Gavin was two years old and my daughter Renee was seven years old. Night after night, she had seen me waiting for her father to show up for dinner, and he never did. It was such a trying time in our lives. I remember the day I moved out, being at Margi's house, moving some stuff over there before we went to the city, San Francisco, to stay for the night. I spoke to another sister, Brooke, on the phone and she asked if I was all right. I said, "I feel like the blinders have come off me, now that I am out."

I had been emoting so much, and feeling so much sadness, that now I could see more clearly, like I had been washing away the illusion of what I was living in. My awareness had shifted and I could see clearly for the first time that what I had just undertaken was the right thing to do. I saw my marriage for the truth of what it was. It could not support me, or the kids, emotionally, and it was the right decision to leave.

I was totally supported in making this change in my life. I had to start thinking about how I would make this work and who I would live with. I needed a roommate, because I could not afford to live on my own. And then, lo and behold, the mom of one of my daughter's best friends (Mary, who was also my good friend) was doing the same thing in her marriage. She was getting a divorce because her husband was not supporting her son, Russ, in his hearing loss and the choice she had made to teach him to be verbal.

She had been commuting from Chico, California, to attend the school both our children were enrolled in, the Jean Weingarten Peninsula Oral School for the Deaf, (JWPOSD), in Belmont, California. This is an amazing school that teaches deaf kids to speak, and it is where Mary and I met. I heard she was moving to HMB and decided to ask if she would like to room together and share expenses. I wasn't sure how it would work out. We rented a wonderful home on Kehoe Avenue, right by the ocean, and merged our families. This was another magical time, the ability to have the support of other kids and another woman who was undergoing a transformation just like mine.

I remember, I decided to have a housewarming party and bring in a shaman (a student of mine) to perform a shaman ritual to sweep negative energy out of the home. We had people coming from HMB and San Francisco, and all over. We all participated in the ritual. When you walked outside, there was a long line of shoes on the sidewalk, as everyone had taken off their shoes when they entered our home. I'll never forget that. It was a ritual of honoring our new beginning – our new family experience – and opening to what we might learn in the process.

For the first time in my life I had experienced what it was like to be held in community and supported in my efforts, loved from the inside out. Renee, Gavin and I will never forget the deep, soul-filled experience of our chosen family there, for it made us who we are today. It changed our perception of the world and community as we knew it, and we have been living from that perception ever since.

My journey had been a culmination of learning how to listen to my body, mind and heart, and how to integrate and merge these aspects of myself. In doing this, I have remembered the essence of who I am, and as a result, I bring my strengths and purpose to my work in the world.

My hope for you is that this book will ignite a deeper conversation within yourself about the aspects of body, mind and heart in you, and how you are choosing to work with them in your life to create the happiness you desire.

Chapter 1: Body Wisdom

In this section, we will talk about the importance of listening to your body, and how, if you do, you can uncover hidden gems that tell you what is working and not working in aligning yourself to that which makes you happy.

FEAR

"Everything you want is on the other side of fear."
– Jack Canfield

Fear is all in how you perceive it and the power you choose to give to it. I believe we are here to experience a life well lived, to take advantage of our bodies as the houses of our soul, and to allow ourselves to explore, revel, linger and be adventurous. We are here to experience all the great capacities of being human, and know that we are being directed by the soul. In this, we remember that we are love, and through this remembering, to know we are not the ones completely in charge of our lives. Rather, we are in a dance with something bigger than ourselves. We are merely a being that is housing a consciousness, and we are here to assist in the development of the consciousness of the planet. In so doing, we have to develop our own consciousness by working on our own growth. We don't even really have to "work" on it, but just give it more attention. We want to allow ourselves to move into the acceptance of who we are and all we are creating, the good and the uncomfortable. We must pay attention to all that is going on emotionally, physically and mentally.

When you can love these three aspects of yourself, you will be living an integrated life. You are here to learn to do this while you are in human form: to be able to integrate all these aspects of yourself in order to live fully. Many people are living one-dimensional lives, from only their heads. What about the other dimensions? We need to drop the blinders, drop all the resistances, and allow ourselves to merge all three of these aspects: body, mind and heart.

We first need to be aware that fear lives in our head, but can show up in a number of ways in our bodies. The mind reflects the body and the body reflects the mind. I would like you to think about how fear shows up in your body. It can present itself as stress, anxiety, tightness in the chest or shoulders, any number of ways. The important thing is to notice where you feel uncomfortable in your body, and to stop and ask yourself: What is your body trying to tell you?

When you do this, you begin by shifting your perspective from siloed (in separate parts) to inclusive. You must learn to collaborate with all aspects of yourself. I believe we are all one. In order to get that experience, we have to align the body, mind and heart. Imagine how that would feel, having your mind, body, and heart working in perfect unison. I imagine it to feel effortless, easy, and in the flow. I imagine it to be full of light and joy and connectedness, where you are able to trust both the unknown and the known, with a body that is stress free.

You are capable of so much more than you ever knew. You are capable of expanding beyond your current reach, beyond what you can imagine. Think about how different your life would be with a simple shift in perception and the courage to move through whatever feels uncomfortable in your physical body.

You have to constantly allow your perception to shift, and remain open, even at the risk of being hurt. In this openness, healing happens. It is where your awareness allows for more veils of illusion to drop, more awareness to be had, and more opening of your heart.

> "We can only heal at the level of consciousness of which we are aware." – Rochelle Schiek

In all the recommendations I get from clients, the one that is repeated over and over again is that I have a unique perspective. This was a driving force in getting me to write this book, realizing that sharing my perspective could serve as positive growth for myself and others. I look at everything as an opportunity to teach me. I choose to feel all my feelings, and get curious with myself.

As I write this book, I notice that I have a strain in my lower-right back area, and I make the connection that this physical message has to do with my identity in the world. This makes sense – as I am moving from coach to author – and building an entire new brand and messaging platform to launch the book. Some aspect of myself, though it may not be conscious to me, is resistant to this change and tightening up. As we will discuss in the chapter on masculine and feminine aspects of yourself, this part of me represents my ability to let go in unknown territory. With this information, I now have the ability to work with this part of my body in a way that will support it in letting go of its grip on me and the change that is occurring.

I want to be the vehicle, and listen to what my body is telling me, because I choose to see my body as a messenger for my own growth. When you start seeing this perspective and applying it, it allows for more ease. The blinders drop and a softening happens, a deepening in your inner being from the inside out. It is learning to be more gentle with yourself, more aware of how to lead yourself and your family, and more loving when physical injury occurs.

I want to support people in shifting their perspective in this direction. I want you to be aware of the resources that are right in front of you, and learn to listen and care for this aspect of yourself.

There is a part of our culture that believes we have to power through no matter how we feel, and that we have to control the outcome. The truth is that this is an illusion. The more you listen to your body and include this aspect of yourself in driving your decisions, the more ease and grace you will experience. There is a cultural belief that it is important to struggle and stay the victim, to not allow yourself to receive the gentleness and care required to create what you really want now. Any time you are pushing through, it is important to notice whether it is supporting your growth, especially when it comes to your physical body, or holding you back.

Listening to your body wisdom keeps you present to your choice to enjoy the journey, and not focus only on the destination – but also to nurture and care for your body during the journey of your life. It is your perception that changes your experience and what you are capable of creating.

I want to give you an example of how I got stuck in my perspective years ago. I had a conversation with my sister Rachel while I was struggling to support my two kids. She told me to look for another job that would pay more. This led me to my first headhunting job. I was making $35K a year, working part time, and I was stuck in the perception that there was no other work that would give me what I have in our small coastal town where I lived. I was feeling grateful that I was given health insurance as a part-time employee.

My boss worked around my kids' schedule and my teaching schedule, and we got along. It was a great environment. It took someone with a different vantage point, like my sister Rachel, to say, "Why don't you see what is out there?" I happened to mention in one of my yoga classes, that I was looking for work, and one of my students happened to know of a high-tech recruiting firm that had opened nearby and wanted to hire another headhunter. I got the job.

They more than doubled my income, while still giving me a great schedule. Miracles abounded. It took my sister sharing her perspective, and me listening and taking action, to create this life change for myself and my family. Sometimes another's perspective is what helps breathe new life into our own, and gives us the ability to make a shift that empowers and enlivens us.

"We don't simply fall into situations accidentally, but create them around ourselves based on our beliefs about reality. If we closely examine aspects of ourselves which are unsatisfactory, we can see that each uncomfortable or unworkable situation serves to show us our own misconceptions and mistaken attitudes. Once we have seen these for what they are, we can correct them or let them go."
–Gerd Ziegler

How often do you take advantage of another's perspective and try it on for yourself? Sometimes it is important to give yourself some breathing room and listen to what your body is telling you in order to help shift your perception. This supports you in moving through your fears and living in more trust, grace and ease.

Breath

"The Breath is the tender charge of God" – Yogi Bhajan

When I heard this, it changed everything for me. I realized that God is with me all the time – and by God, I mean that which is bigger than me (so call it whatever you need or wish to). It was a reminder to use my breath to bring in the divine aspect of myself, to ignite my intuition and inner knowing. All of a sudden, it gave meaning to why we want to expand our breath capacity and our ability to breathe. The breath is what sustains us. When we die, we stop breathing and many of us believe our souls leave our bodies. For me, one strategy or touchstone, as I like to call it, is focusing more on my breath to feel more connected to my inner guide.

There are so many important breathing exercises. Long, deep breathing expands the lung capacity. It cleans out toxins in your system, calms your nervous system, and changes the pH balance of the blood. It expands your thinking and your capacity, and it nurtures you. It is a tonic for the nervous system in that it calms you and gives you space from your thinking. It creates momentum for you to achieve your goals. Breath is Divine in nature and we often don't treat it that way.

What can you do to begin to put attention on your breath? The best way to begin to understand the power of your breath is to make time to breathe. Allow the simple act of breathing to show you things about yourself that you may not be aware of. If you choose to believe that breath is the tender charge of God, then you are never really alone – as the presence of God is with you as long as you are breathing. So, when you are feeling anxious, overwhelmed, scared, create a reminder or touchstone for yourself to start putting attention on your breath.

I had a client who noticed that she would get anxious in certain company meetings, and her touchstone was a sticky note she put on her computer that said BREATHE. This was her reminder that when she was feeling uncomfortable, she started long, deep breathing. It would shift how she experienced the meeting in a positive way. She kept it on her computer so she could remember, throughout her day, anytime she felt her negative thinking coming on or stress in her body, that breathing would help. That sticky note supported her in creating the pattern in her mind and her body to start breathing long and deep in situations where her body or mind was in reaction. As you try this, just notice what begins to happen in your mind and how you begin to feel in your body. Observe yourself without any judgment.

Breath is the food for the body and the sensory system, the mind and the heart. Breath is all-encompassing. By focusing on your breathing, you help to shift your perception and your awareness. The breath can be your guide to how you are feeling. It helps you open, expand, and breathe into more of what you are capable.

Breath is your life force, and it sustains you from the inside out. It recalibrates you and keeps you living and functioning. "Breath of fire" is another transformative breath exercise. It is a key tool for activating your navel center, which is the seat of your power in the energy system. It expands the lung capacity and it clears the auric field (the subtle energy that surrounds our bodies). The clearer your auric field, the more clearly you connect with your soul. There are components to the breath that we are not even aware of. I love this description of it from the book, *The Tree of Yoga* by B.K.S. Iyengar.

PRANAYAMA

As leaves aerate a tree and provide nourishment for its healthy growth, so pranayama feeds and aerates the cells, nerves, organs and intelligence, and consciousness of the human system. When performing a posture, we can only extend the body fully if we synchronize the breath with the movement.

Prana is energy; Ayama is creation, distribution and maintenance. Pranayama is the science of breath, which leads to the creation, distribution and maintenance of vital energy.

Pranayama is the bridge between the physical and the spiritual – it is the hub of yoga.

The regulation of the breath keeps the respiratory gate clean and open, and through an unobstructed, undisturbed circulatory system, the blood feeds each and every part of our body. By allowing the blood to circulate to the areas of the body which are unhealthy, they are nourished; toxins are dissolved and the various ailments and symptoms of physical diseases can come to an end. This may take place over a long period of time. It is a natural process and operates at the rhythm of natural processes.

Breath is a powerful, subtle force that resides inside everyone and that you have access to all the time, whenever you want. It helps you laugh and feel joy, and it helps you cry and sob and feel your heart. Breathe into the heart and know that you are held; you are a part of something subtle and powerful. I find it amazing to think this – that we are more scared of our power than our weakness. If we just put attention on these elements, we can change the chemistry of our body, our brains, and our heart. This is so important to be aware of and to observe in yourself.

Where do you breathe from, your belly or your chest? How long can you hold your breath in, and how long can you hold your breath out? What is your relationship with your own breath? To your own connection? To your creator? How can you strengthen that connection?

Your body and your breath are one. I had a yoga teacher who said this all the time, and it felt good to hear as a reminder. Your breath is what keeps you connected to your source – the divine within you – and it keeps you alive. Breath opens the space for you to learn to *be* instead of *do*.

Breathing Exercises:

Exercise #1:
Begin by taking in a long, deep breath through your nose and breathing in from your belly. When you are at full lung capacity, slightly suspend the breath and then slowly let it out through your nose. Practice for three minutes.
Notice what it shifts in your head, and how you feel in your body.

Exercise #2:
Take a long, deep breath in through your nose and suspend it for as long as you can, slowly exhale out through the nose and suspend the breath out as long as is comfortable, so you can then inhale slowly. Continue this cycle for three minutes.
Notice what you experience and where you experience comfort with your breath, and where you experience discomfort.
Holding the breath in affects the sympathetic nervous system (the nerves which put the body "on alert" and stimulate us) and can temporarily raise the blood pressure. Holding the breath out affects the parasympathetic nervous system (the nerves that relax the body) and temporarily lowers the blood pressure.
– Yogi Bhajan

The more your breath capacity expands, the more comfortable it will be to suspend the breath and hold the breath in as well as out. I invite you to make a practice of breathing, daily or weekly. Just start with a time that works for you. You will begin to notice its subtle and powerful effects. At work during the day, you think better and begin to come up with solutions to the toughest problems automatically by engaging your breath in moments of stress or anxiety or negative thinking. It is great to practice anytime and anywhere, but especially in times when you are thinking negatively, feeling stress or being challenged by external situations.

Giving yourself a pause to breathe and do nothing eases stress, calms the nervous system and opens the mind to allow stillness to enter. I love the feeling of stillness. There is nothing more nurturing to me than sitting in stillness. Whether I am in nature, in my office or when I am meditating, it creates the space for me to listen deeply and observe what is in front of me and inside of me.

The art of "not doing" is so pleasurable to my senses, and it makes me feel so calm and relaxed. I love not doing and I practice it as often as I can. In a society where so many of us are addicted to doing, the art of not doing is a wonderful way to bring balance to your brain, relax your body and ease your stress.

Perhaps if we gave up doing, we would experience more being. What is one thing you could give up and make space for not doing? Doing nothing, absolutely nothing, I think even just ten minutes a day would be helpful for anyone. This practice of doing nothing gives the mind permission to do what it needs to do and gives you the opportunity to not get caught up in your thoughts.

We create a thousand thoughts per wink of the eye, according to Yogi Bhajan. There is no such thing as stopping thoughts. The trick is to not get caught up in them and, instead, just watch them come in and go out, as if they were a movie screen in your mind's eye. Then focus on the space between the thoughts. The more attention you put on the space between your thoughts, the more that space will grow inside your mind and thoughts will begin to be background noise and not front and center. This calms the noise inside your head and gives you an experience of deep peace.

Eventually, you no longer get engaged in the ripples and the thoughts. You become still in the middle of the movement. How cool is that! I like to describe this as being the stone Buddha in the center of Las Vegas. If you can, picture yourself as a stone Buddha sitting in the center of your busy life. Think of Vegas, where there are so many BSOs (bright, shiny objects) to distract you. You are a pillar of strength in the midst of all the challenges and chaos in your life, yet you are focused on the space inside yourself instead of the fear that lives in your head.

This is what cultivating internal stillness creates: though you are in the middle of chaos, you stay calm and centered in yourself so that you can make the best choice at the time without getting distracted by what is external. This is when you begin to listen to your inner guide – and the more you act on what that guidance is telling you, the more you trust yourself. This builds confidence from the inside out.

If you are constantly testing the latest fad and moving from one thing to the next, you may find this challenging initially, but with practice, you will reap the rewards. If you like to control everything and keep *doing* no matter what, you will find that allowing stillness and space will give you more energy, but from a calm, relaxed place. Imagine how it would feel to be the strong pillar in the center of challenges, change and chaos in your life. This is what meditation develops, and I am sure there are other practices that develop this as well. The key is putting attention on your internal stillness, for this creates awareness of it and invokes the practice of being still.

Begin by just noticing how often you choose to be still, versus doing and going, and notice how you feel and what thoughts come to your mind when you want to distract yourself with doing.

I know I have a hard time doing this. It helps to put attention on it daily and make it a habit. I feel as though sometimes I don't know the answer or direction to take on a particular work project or personal obstacle, and I just have to stop, pause, and breathe deep. This helps me to center – and then I visualize the stone Buddha in the middle of Vegas. I am a visual learner, and so images are great touchstones for me when starting a new practice. The image helps me to notice my feeling and allow myself to actually feel it.

An easy practice to start is to set aside ten minutes a day, ideally in the morning before your day starts, to just sit with a straight spine, eyes closed and attention focused in at the seat between your eyebrows. This is the energetic center of your intuition, and it's called the "third eye" in yogic practices. By merely focusing there, you activate your intuition and begin to strengthen your inner voice. Why do we want to activate it? Because the more we strengthen our intuition, the more we trust ourselves. The more we trust ourselves, the more peace and happiness we experience.

If ten minutes is hard, start with five minutes; if that is hard, start with three minutes. In the silence, we can hear the divine. In the silence we can hear our inner knowing. In the silence, we can rest and make room for the heart to speak. In the silence is the space of the heart – perhaps that is why I love it so much. It makes me feel so at peace and fulfilled, no matter what may be going on in my work or my life.

In the silence, you learn to listen deeply, you can hear your own heart beat and you learn to love all aspects of yourself. In the silence, you can master your mind. If you meet your thoughts with silence and stillness, in time you no longer become enrolled in them to take your attention and energy. When you meet anything with reaction, you move into control and fear – and this is from the mind, not the heart. Fear lives in the mind – and love lives in the heart.

You are made up of heart space, mind space, and body space, and by bringing stillness and silence into each of these aspects of yourself, you begin to integrate them inside yourself. This creates an internal congruency which gives the experience of pure stillness. Using the breath as a tool is the key for me. Deep breathing gives you the space and permission to witness yourself and to develop the observer mind and notice who you truly are. In doing this, you begin to recognize your truth – and this ignites your creative genius, remembering your true essence and even more, what will make you deeply happy.

Reinvention

"Life isn't about finding yourself; it is about creating yourself." – George Bernard Shaw

I moved from my career to my calling eight years ago, unaware that coaching would be my career path. I had an idea of what I wanted, which was supporting others in living authentic lives that are true to who they are, but I had no clue as to how that would happen. Coaching found me when Gavin was in high school. He was a junior, and I decided that I wanted to reinvent myself. He would be in college in one year and that small voice inside me was loud and clear that it was time to make a transition into work that filled me.

I had been successful headhunting but I was sick of it. It felt soulless. I had done it for twelve years, helping CEOs find executive talent, but I wasn't part of helping the organization be systemically better; I just provided talent. The candidates I placed would come back to me and to talk through issues they were having with their executive leadership after I placed them.

I realized one day while talking to a candidate about his issues with the CEO that this was the type of conversation I wanted to continue having with people. The candidate and I would discuss a strategy for communicating with the CEO, and once he did that, the issue was solved. That is what I wanted to get paid for, and the idea prompted me to talk to a coach. I spoke with my sister one day about my dilemma, and she said. "Do you want to chat with a coach I am working with? Maybe you will gain some clarity." It was a free session, so what could it hurt? In that thirty-minute call I uncovered my next step, to explore the idea of coaching as a profession.

I interviewed coaches to see what schools they went to, asked questions specific to what my needs and desires were, and made my decision to start coaching. I signed up at Coach U – and the rest is history. I built my business, while continuing to do recruiting work, and now, eight years later, I am coaching full time – and I have never looked back. I spent five years focusing on my marketing efforts, and three years ago, all the pieces fell in place with the model I have now, that allows me a full schedule of coaching clients. And this project appeared: writing a book to share what I have learned in creating both a career and a life that I love.

My creativity continues to grow in ways I never expected. I created the amazing home I live in; I created this amazing career where I can work virtually from anywhere in the world and make a great income. I attracted the most amazing clients and colleagues to work with. I want this for everyone: to believe that you can create your heart's desire, to trust that your heart knows where and when to direct you, to listen to the still voice inside you that knows all – and to let that voice guide you. You have to trust yourself to take the necessary steps to follow your divine guidance to grow your potential with your family and friends, and in your work. When we are fully engaged in the creation process of our lives, we become magnetic, and this feels fulfilling.

I feel plugged into a force greater than myself. I feel empowered, supported and open to what shows up, and I feel so grateful to be given this time and space to practice, work, love, laugh, and support the shift of the consciousness of the planet. I like to call myself a Gardener of Consciousness. Most importantly, I feel comfortable and confident in my own skin. I trust myself. This is the legacy I want to leave – that I learned to integrate with the Divine, I learned to work with all the parts of myself and I learned to love myself fully. I learned that my being here mattered. Mind you, this didn't come without learning how to work with my resistance. This is an ongoing lesson for me.

As I have already discussed in previous chapters, we cannot tap into this deep inner knowing without creating space for stillness of mind and body. In the stillness our consciousness is cultivated. In the stillness, we experience the garden of our hearts and allow our consciousness to flower in the world. It is in this space where we allow ourselves to meet all of us, the dark and the light within ourselves, and to honor both. What distracts you from being a gardener of your own consciousness? What I have learned is that looking at our darkness is as important as looking at our light – and resistance is a great teacher working with us to learn to love even deeper.

Resistance

"What you resist, persists." – C.G. Jung

I find that resisting the temptation to give in to whatever we are resisting takes a lot more energy than just surrendering to it and allowing it. We are trained to resist at such an early age that it becomes part of who we are, and of who we think we are. It is an automatic response. I invite you to think about taking the power of resistance and turning it into surrender instead. I smile just thinking about it. I imagine it feels like floating on a raft down a river, and letting my body totally relax and be carried by the water.

When I was in Mexico once, I came upon a hammock that was hung over the ocean, and it was rocked by the waves that rolled in. All you had to do was lie there and allow yourself to be rocked. Rocked by Mother Nature. No wonder babies like to be rocked; it is in our nature to be held and rocked to the rhythm of the mother. It feels relaxing just thinking about it. Let me give you some examples of how resistance shows up.

We have resistance with other people, like the guy at the office who has to have the last word on every topic. What if you let him have his way and worked with your resistance to the point that it no longer bothered you? How different would your experience be? What can you start surrendering to right now in your work or your life? Pick one thing and give yourself over to it no matter what anyone thinks.

Think about a person or situation that shows up at work that makes you mad, or pushes your button – and rather than pushing against it by judging it, being defensive or sarcastic, or feeling as if you have to justify yourself, try to just allow yourself to notice the feeling you are feeling and let it be there without acting on it. This is surrendering into resistance.

Just allow yourself to fall into what you are resisting. Immerse yourself in whatever feeling it is that bothers you. This kind of surrender into an uncomfortable feeling cultivates loving kindness with ourselves and with each other. It requires being open to changing your view from giving up to giving over, and releasing the grip of the mind. It is a way to change the circuitry in the brain and create a new brain pattern and behavior that serves you, rather than works against you. I have noticed that a lot of people communicate from a place of defensiveness versus curiosity, when it comes to challenges in communication at work.

When your buttons get pushed, you notice it hurts, and if you go into "reaction mode," even if you don't think you are taking it personally, subconsciously you are. By leaning into resistance, you are able to pause, stay present with how you feel, notice it and then bring your attention back to the other party. Then listen to that person objectively, and from there, respond in a way that serves your growth. All of this happens in a split second, as you begin to bring attention and practice to it. This is all a part of developing your emotional intelligence.

Emotional intelligence (commonly referred to as EI or EQ) burst onto the business scene with the publication of journalist and psychologist Daniel Goleman's best-selling book, *Emotional Intelligence,* in 1995. The definition of emotional intelligence that is offered by Mayer, Salovey and Caruso (2000, p. 396) is "the ability to perceive and express emotion, assimilate emotion in thought, understand and reason with emotion, and regulate emotion in the self and others." Above all, skills to learn as a leader of teams, companies and yourself, it is emotional intelligence. By strengthening your EQ, you rise to the top in all areas of your life. A lot of what I am speaking to in this book is related to doing just this – putting attention on the emotional aspect of yourself.

You have heard me talk about touchstones or strategies for changing your behavior and supporting you in rewiring your brain, and helping you remember to practice these new techniques. For me, mantras have been one of my touchstones, a miraculous system of support when it comes to reprogramming my thoughts. I use mantras from the Yogi Bhajan's Kundalini

Yoga and Meditation tradition, because I have studied them and know what they mean, and have practiced them for over twenty years. I fell into a class over thirty years ago; I loved it and never looked back.

> "A Mantra is nothing more than a collection of words strung together to create a positive effect."
> – Robin S. Sharma

I know they work because it has been proved to me by watching their impact on my kids. When I was pregnant with Gavin, I chanted a mantra every day for happiness and holiness – it is a beautiful chant.

> Guru Guru Wahe Guru, Guru Ram Das Guru
> Guru – teacher or guide that brings one from the darkness to the light.
> Wahe – exclamation of ecstasy like "WOW!"
> Ram Das – literally translates as "God's Servant,"
> and Guru Ram Das also refers to the Fourth Guru of the Sikhs

This mantra was given to Yogi Bhajan by Guru Ram Das when he was in a meditative state. As Guru Ram Das, the fourth Guru of the Sikhs, he was known for his humility and healing abilities. This mantra is also known for its healing qualities and for imparting humility to the one who chants it. This mantra relates directly to the healing and protective energy represented by Guru Ram Das. The mantra is composed of two parts. The first part is a nirgun mantra (Guru Guru Wahe Guru). This projects the mind to the source of knowledge and ecstasy. The second part is a sirgun mantra (Guru Ram Das Guru). This refers to the wisdom that comes as a servant of the infinite. It is the mantra of humility. It reconnects the experience of the finite to infinity.

When Gavin was born, I was the only one in the room, and I started chanting the chant while he was breastfeeding for the first time. At one point, he stopped feeding and looked up at me with the biggest smile. He recognized the vibration. It was comfort and assurance for him that he was okay in this stark environment, fresh out of the womb. Then, when he was fifteen years old, I played the chant again, a different version of it, and he came down the stairs and said, "I don't know why, but I love this chant." (This was at an age when he used to say, "Don't play that chanting music when my friends come over.") I told him, "I know why you like it," and I told him the story. The mantras are sacred phrases – expressed usually in the Hindi or Sanskrit language, in Gurmukhi script, as in the discipline of Kundalini Yoga. And like all our words, they hold a certain vibration or energy, like a radio wave.

All words hold a vibration, which is why it is important for us to be conscious of what we are saying. These mantras hold the vibration of the lineage of saints, gurus and sages throughout the ages, sacred holiness and vibration and reverence. The sound current goes into our body and reprograms our consciousness. Here is a description of how it works as it relates to the practice of the Kundalini yoga discipline.

The highest nerve endings in the body are in our hearts, head, hands, feet and thighs (this is the largest area of bone marrow and the largest producer of red blood cells). The heart teaches us we must exert to give and relax to receive. You receive until you overflow, then you exude because you're overflowing. In the heart, the attitude of the mantra is being imprinted in the blood cells. Kundalini Yoga is a practice that integrates your body, mind and heart.

The number of minutes you practice a meditation or mantra is equal to the number of heart beats that populate the blood cells and the maximum number of blood cells that have the attitude of the meditation you are practicing. The blood carries the intention of the meditation all the time. The heart is 100 times more electromagnetic than the brain. This intention goes into the blood, where there is a high iron content, to magnetize and reprogram the body.

Once this divine sound is in our cells, it restructures the other cells, and the cells shift the consciousness of the body and behavior. By listening to chanting, we are changing the consciousness of the body and thus the awareness of ourselves and our lives. My kids grew up with chants and would occasionally chant. Just by listening to them, it reprogrammed their brain to a higher thought wave.

My daughter Renee rowed competitively in high school and college. She could not wear her cochlear implants on the water, so she was without sound. To focus and not be distracted by the fear of not being able to hear anything and the stress of wanting to win the race, she would internally chant this one chant, called the protective mantra.

> AD GURAY NAMEH, JUGAD GURAY NAMEH,
> SAT GURAY NAMEH, SIRI GURU DEVAY NAMEH

This comes from the ancient script, the Mangala Charn Mantra, and it is chanted for protection. It surrounds the magnetic field with protective light, and means, "I bow to the primal Guru (guiding consciousness who takes us to God-Realization), I bow to wisdom through the ages, I bow to True Wisdom, I bow to the great, unseen wisdom."

Renee said it was like she was transported during the race. When she started out, she was very nervous. Once she got in the boat, though, she got into the vibration of the chant, and out of her head where the fear lives, and before she knew it, she was across the finish line. She was a national champion in her last year in high school – first time ever for this crew to win a national championship race. Her vibration alone helped the other girls in the boat get in the same step, even though they were not internally chanting. That is what it does when we shift our own internal dialogue. When we shift our vibration, we make an energetic wave – and it can shift a boat, a room, a family and a business.

Little did I know at the time that while I was struggling with my own resistances of reprogramming my own internal dialogue, I was putting this software into my two young children's brains – and that it would serve them today in living authentically to their truth and to the truth of who they are. Our journey here has a miraculous ability to show us the way, and it is our job to pay attention, trust the signs and follow our instinct, and our hearts – for this always leads to grace.

Grace

It is no coincidence that we use the word grace both to describe physical beauty of movement and for a state of spiritual blessedness. When life-energy flows in its fullness through any living being, it manifests internally as pleasure and externally as grace.

Grace and pleasure are natural attributes of the sacred. Every time you ignore what gives your body pleasure, you lose some of the grace that every child and every wild animal possesses in such abundance.

Grace is a wonderful word, one of the few in the English language that stands at the intersection of the physical and the spiritual, reminding us that our task as human beings is not simply to identify ourselves as spiritual beings, but to embody spirit. Grace is the fruit of such embodiment. – Jalaja Bonheim, Ph.D., Author and Speaker

Experiencing grace is such a moment of magic. I experienced grace this morning, staring at the sunrise from my bedroom window. It was so amazing and beautiful and otherworldly, it took me all the way into the center of my heart. I felt like this time, right now, will never be repeated. This time is a once-in a-lifetime moment, and this time is worthy of being present to it.

Sometimes resistance is a natural part of the process that helps us move into grace – it teaches us to relax and let go. It teaches us to move into our heart and out of our head; it teaches us to allow and not worry about the outcome. That is a big part of being human, since we worry a lot about the outcomes. Worry is putting attention on what you don't want. Let go of worry and just be present in the moment. Melt into the tension of letting the resistance go. There is a mystery in the universe and it is our part to learn how to trust it and allow it.

This creates magic, for it supports us in believing that we are love. This allows our heart to open, to feel words someone says or an action someone takes towards us – and it allows them to come all the way into our hearts. When you feel this experience all the way in, you experience another part of the world and another part of yourself. In this state of being, the resistance dissolves – and when the resistance dissolves, the words will flow and all will be well.

You can choose to be a victim, or you can choose to allow the experience to take over you – being fully aware, and present, and welcoming to the sensations and feelings. It is your choices that create the direction of your life. You can choose to create grace or resistance. Which experiences are showing up most often for you? Listening to your heart supports you in experiencing more grace while you are here, and supports you in embracing another aspect of your subtle body, the feminine aspect of yourself.

Chapter 2: Mindful Matters

I want to transition now to bring attention and awareness to your mind, the mental aspect of yourself. As we go through these topics, please remember that you are the only one you have control over – and it is the choices you make about how you think that have an impact on how the body responds and what you create in your life. Your thoughts create the reflection of what you are seeing in your life. Let's explore a way of using that to serve your growth.

A key component of learning what relaxes you and gives you breathing space is to simply begin to observe yourself without judgment. Just notice what you hear, see and feel without putting any meaning on it. This practice will support you in learning how not to judge, or compare yourself to others. And as a result, it will allow you to live true to who you are and share your strengths with others.

> The practice of mindfulness is learning how to live your life deeply so you don't waste your life.
> – Thich Nhat Hanh

Masculine & Feminine

When we hear the words "masculine" and "feminine," I want you to understand that we are speaking of energy, and both these energies lie in all beings. Masculine energy can be defined as a supporting energy, protecting and caring energy, more action-oriented. The feminine energy, on the other side, is a caring, nurturing and extremely nourishing energy; it is the energy of receiving. The masculine is the "doing" while the feminine is the "being." When it relates to the body in the energetic system, the right side of the body is considered masculine and the left side feminine.

For example, wedding rings are worn on the left ring finger because this side and this finger is associated with a meridian that connects to the heart. A meridian is a channel in the energetic system that energy flows through. If you can begin to view your body as energy, you begin to see a more holistic picture of what you really have access to in the way of communication with your body.

If I had to capsulate my life, I would say that my journey has been learning about the masculine and the feminine, and how to integrate these two aspects of myself. How to honor both, develop both and live in a balanced state with both. My masculine and feminine are always evolving, and right now I am learning another level of the feminine by letting my fingers be guided in what to write in this book. The feminine aspect of myself allows me to trust the process and let the words flow. Just as we have a left brain, which is more analytical, and a right brain, which generates more creative abilities, we have these two forms of energy.

For the heart is where everything flowers, it is in the heart where I feel elevated and open, in the heart I feel the depth of emotion to be able to give this book meaning. Your heart is the key to your body; without it we are walking sticks. That is what John and I used to call people who were not in touch with both heart and soul, Walking Sticks. I used to love the conversations he and I would have after we went to bed, and all the lights were out and it was dark. We would first brag about how amazing the kids were, and then we had these spiritual conversations.

I loved that part of our day and our marriage. It filled me up and helped me feel connected to him, and to something bigger. Most of the time, while I was raising the kids, we lived in a very spiritually connected community of people. I love the feeling of living in community and always having community around. It was so comforting for me as a single mom. It was so nurturing and healthy for me to be accepted for who I was as a single mom.

I experienced the truth of the statement, "It takes a village to raise a child." I feel that my time in HMB, California was like no other. It restructured so much of my family-of-origin conditioning, and so much of my life and beliefs, and it was such a struggle. I was depressed for so long that finally, when things shifted, starting on my fortieth year, I finally began to feel I was gaining some ground and had survived the roughest patch. I can say that I have achieved the integrated life of the masculine and feminine, because I chose to take on the task of learning how to care and support my family – specifically, developing my masculine.

I also learned how to activate my feminine nature and learn how to receive and love myself more deeply. I continue to learn more about this aspect of myself every day.

With all of this, I continued to dive into my heart for guidance and do my soul work. In being committed to a daily practice of this work, it grew in me the ability to integrate both of these aspects of myself. This morning, I sat down and read Rochelle Schieck's blog about the new moon. It is a new moon in Libra, which is all about integrating the masculine and feminine energies. How appropriate it is for me to be writing this in acknowledgment of myself, and how I have accomplished that in my own life. My spiritual name, given to me when I became a teacher of Kundalini Yoga and Meditation

(Yogi Bhajan's teachings), is RAM RATTAN KAUR, precious jewel that creates the sun and the moon.

My interpretation of this name has been to anchor both the masculine and feminine qualities in my own self, and to share my journey and learnings with the world – and it has supported me in mentally understanding my process within my body. It is important to remember that you have to integrate your physical, emotional and mental aspects of yourself in order to fully anchor yourself in new learning and awarenesses that will support you in living a happy life. This starts by observing yourself.

Self-Observation

"The highest spiritual practice is self-observation without judgment." Swami Kripalu

Now, we'll focus on how to observe ourselves, and cultivate the observer in our own being. By learning to observe yourself, you are then able to cultivate the neutral mind, the part of yourself that watches with loving kindness and stops judging and comparing yourself to others. To be able to go into an observer state, you have to practice being non-judgmental of yourself. You have to drop your neurosis and learn to just allow and notice and not take anything personally. This is hard to do when you are reacting instead of responding.

Reacting is another form of resisting, and it is a natural part of the process. As I write this book, I experience all kinds of resistance. My left brain is asking, why am I writing this book? Why is this so important to me? Why does it matter?

I could have gone hiking and relaxed this weekend. But that would not be putting myself in the zone of the divine, and moving into more of my potential – and that is the dilemma. We resist expanding our potential. This is what I am noticing about myself. Because stepping into more of my potential requires loving myself more deeply, and bringing more of my gifts to the world. We resist loving ourselves more deeply.

By being the observer, I am able to relax and realize I am not part of this, that I am just a conduit for the words to come out. I am only the vessel for the divine, to enter me and the paper I'm writing on, for this power bigger than myself to take hold of my fingers. This is where integration of head and heart happen. When you begin to put time into observing yourself, you begin to shift your perception of yourself – and all of life.

Be aware, and notice what your voice says to you when you are quiet. Notice if it feels uncomfortable, or pleasant. Take note of the words your mind is speaking to you. Is it calm, like a gentle tide, or a constant negative chatter and a worry?

If it is constant chatter, you want to put your attention into relaxing the body and mind. I relax my body and mind through foot reflexology, a walk in nature or a hike. I can feel at times as if I have all this energy bottled up, and it just needs to be released. Once I move my body, then I can rest in myself and be more present in my focus. Self-care is about feeling good, feeling joy and feeling at peace.

To be able to rest, you need to care for yourself. What does it mean to care for self? Loving yourself, being able to give to yourself in a way that induces relaxation, joy and pleasure. Each of us experiences this in a different way. There is no singular right way. Make note of one action you can take today that will help you rest in yourself. Start your practice of observation, and see what awareness it awakens in you.

It is important to listen to what works for you. It is different for all of us. We all have different experiences, and have done different things with our bodies, so each of us needs unique things that will help us relax and feel peace. What is that for you? I love walking in nature by the water. There are simple things I incorporate every day that keep me in a relaxed state. They also help me stay aware and present to what is most important to me, and to remember who I am – and how to love myself.

Sometimes it is a hot lavender bath with Epsom salt. Epsom salt cleans the electromagnetic field around your body. The electromagnetic field is like an energy field that subtly surrounds our bodies. It picks up negativity and stress without our even knowing it. If we have a cluttered field, it is harder to be clear about what we need for ourselves.

Self-care is allowing your heart, instead of your head, to be in the driver's seat. Sometimes it requires surrendering, giving up the to-do list, and allowing your brain to take a break. Be gentle with yourself and start small. It is important to remember that we have to do this more than just when we take a vacation. In order for this to become a habit, we have to incorporate it into our everyday lives. Only then can it integrate into our physical and mental bodies. So, start with one activity a week to begin with, and then build on that as it becomes more comfortable.

It is so easy not to put attention on something so subtle. We must retrain ourselves to be able to take our attention off the distractions of the noise in our lives and direct it to where we find peace, even if that is only three minutes of deep breathing.

It is so easy to focus on what is loud, instead of what is subtle and quiet, like the voice in your heart, like the signs in your body, like the small, still voice in your head. We distract ourselves with what is outside of us, so as not to hear the negative voices in our head. Mine is calm like a calm surf at times, but only when I set attention on it and relax my body.

Through various practices, like foot reflexology, yoga, working out, cardio, sex, a walk, or a hike in nature, you support your mind in calming down, and in aligning your body and heart. Our body signals what is going on in the mind, and they both work in tandem with each other. So if we calm the body, we calm the mind; if we calm the mind, we calm the body. Then you can rest in yourself. This is true self-care. It shows self-love by giving yourself the space to release the tension from your body and mind, to allow you to rest inside your being. Giving to the self, being quiet with the self – this is nurturing the self.

It is different for everyone, as we all have different types of bodies and we each need different things that will help us relax and feel the space inside ourselves. What is it for You?

Here is a list that works for me. I invite you to create your own list of daily delights.

- Lavender & Epsom salt bath
- Yoga
- Meditation
- Working out
- Walking out in nature and by water
- "Tension Tamer" tea while doing nothing
- Naps in the middle of the day
- Taking short dance breaks to my favorite songs in the middle of my work day

All these are simple things I incorporate into my days to help me stay in a relaxed state, where I can be aware and present with myself. These practices help me remember who I am and what is really important in my life. Remember, staying connected to the heart, not the head, is the key to embracing that which is important and subtle in your life.

I think about when I started my Kundalini Yoga practice: I set aside Renee's nap time as my time to care for myself. It was sometimes one hour, sometimes fifteen minutes; it varied, based on the day. I so looked forward to this time for myself. We live in an addictive society, so let's work that to our advantage and do an activity that helps us live in our heart from a state of presence and awareness, instead of doing an activity that doesn't support our growth. In other words, you can create a habit that is healthy for you, serves your growth, and supports you in feeling fulfilled and happy.

We have become addicted as a society to the negative things that don't grow our heart, for instance, reality TV shows, sugar, caffeine, alcohol, work. All these distract us to a point of numbness and unawareness. They keep us from being present. This breaks trust with ourselves, and allows fear to creep in and direct our actions, thoughts, and behaviors.

I find in my work with clients that the majority of people waste so much time doubting where they are going, and not trusting the process. I invite you to begin to trust whatever shows up as an opportunity to teach you something about yourself. I invite you to take time for stillness and observation every day, and to allow these practices to support you in molding your beliefs and behaviors in a direction that serves your growth and the life you want to be living.

As author, philosopher, theologian, educator, and civil rights leader Howard Thurman says, "Don't ask what the world needs. Ask what makes you come alive. Because what the world needs is people who have come alive."

Where in your life do you not feel alive? I feel so alive in my life and so grateful for all the amazing miracles I experience every day, with so much magic to witness. Being a part of this is what helps me feel alive. I feel empowered by my choices, now, when I begin to feel disempowered, I can immediately recognize it and put strategies in place to shift it by listening to myself, finding out what I need in that moment. This is the power of cultivating a keen awareness and trust of your inner self. Let's explore how to work with certain feelings that don't feel empowering.

Through my forgiveness work, John and I will remain friends and family for the rest of our lives, and when we find our significant others, they will come into the fold. It will not be an either/or situation; it will be inclusive. We will all be open to loving each other and being a family that loves. This is the stuff that makes me come alive, and it is how I want to experience my life. This is LOVE. When I think about this part of my journey in awareness, I think of all the guilt I allowed myself to feel, and how much I used it to work against me instead of for me. I need to address the topic of guilt, and how we can use it as our teacher to experience more love of self.

Guilt

"Guilt is anger directed at ourselves – for what we did or did not do." – Peter McWilliams

Guilt is a big topic, and it comes to my mind as a shadow side of ourselves. I like to demonstrate how it serves our growth with a conversation I had with my daughter, Renee, one day. She told me she wished she could go one day without experiencing guilt. I asked her, "You experience guilt every day?" She said "Yes." I was struck at the thought of how stressful and uncomfortable that must be for her.

I asked her, "How is guilt teaching you about yourself?" She responded with, "It's not." I told her that guilt shows up because it is directing us to listen to why we are feeling that way. When guilt shows up, it is teaching you to take the action that makes you feel guilty. If you are feeling guilty for saying "No", it is because you are supposed to say No – whatever the guilt is bringing up is your truth. Use it to do exactly what you feel guilty about. In this way, you are honoring your truth.

It is telling you to take care of yourself. For example, I was dating a guy. We had been on several dates and he wanted to go home with me, but I wasn't ready to sleep with him. I knew he was chomping at the bit. Even though I was feeling guilty in saying no, I said no, I am not ready, and he accepted that. I went home and got into my king-sized bed, and it felt so good to be in my bed alone, to go home alone and not bring him in to my sanctuary. I did not want to start an intimate relationship by going home after a night of a few drinks and shuffleboard – yuck!

Talk about unconscious: I wanted to approach being in a relationship in my life from the place of sacredness, of honoring my body and temple as a woman. By acknowledging my guilt, and doing what I felt guilty about doing, which was saying no to him, I was awakening my feminine power and loving myself. I have lived a life full of taking action out in the world – this is our masculine aspect of ourselves – and by saying NO, I was honoring the feminine aspect of myself, namely, the part of myself, that provided the feeling of guilt to get me to listen to myself.

I invite you to explore these aspects of masculine and feminine in yourself, and see how they show up in your life. In putting attention on them, you have the ability to balance them and deepen their integration in your life – and see everything as your teacher.

Everything as Your Teacher

My work is very fulfilling, because I get to share how to make even the hardest times in your life serve as your teacher. If you choose to look at everything as your teacher, the good and the bad, then your perspective will shift from getting even to being able to hold yourself in love and compassion. This ability creates the realization that everything is always supporting you to grow into more of who you are capable of becoming. How you choose to meet it, and what you choose to do with it, that is another story. I want to address, how you choose to meet the various situations in your life, the good and the challenging, the sad and the happy, the fulfilling and the stagnant aspects.

I want you to know that the truth of every aspect of yourself is powerful, magnificent and beautiful – all aspects are filled with grace and awe. Believing that you hold this magic and choosing to direct your attention towards that belief will support you in leaning into your magnificence much more easily. When you adopt strategies and beliefs that support the essence of who you are, then the trials of life don't sting as much, because you are able to hold yourself in compassion instead of fear.

My children were two of the many gifts from my marriage. I knew when I married John that I would have two kids, one boy and one girl, and that is what happened. And they are a brilliant manifestation of the best of both of us. They are such amazing, aware, compassionate beings, who are willing to look at themselves, be open and have fun, all at the same time.

John reflected for me my own shadow, the parts of myself I had not yet owned up to or fully loved yet. He reflected my own wounded pieces - that I needed time to heal and learn to love. The importance of honoring our reflections is to notice if your actions allow you to love even the parts of yourself that you don't like, to include all the messiness in your life instead of shutting it out. In doing this, you fully love yourself and this allows you to experience an even deeper love.

To learn to love yourself could be the hardest thing you will ever do, only because of your conditioning. If you choose to love yourself, it can be fulfilling, joyous and juicy. Then you can begin to balance your brain, release your fear and stress, and begin to reprogram your thinking towards growth. When you do that, you become an example for others to follow, and this gives them permission to do the same. This creates a positive ripple effect that our world needs.

One of my friends, Paul, asked me one time, "Why do we always say, 'I want to love unconditionally'? He said, "The word, LOVE, is unconditional." This was such a great remark, and one I have taken to heart. Love is unconditional, and it is your mind and your learned behavior that places conditions around your love. These conditions are what activate your fears, doubts and resistances, thus not allowing you to experience love as unconditional. Imagine seeing every relationship in love and with a purpose, to teach you something about yourself. Your interaction with those relationships may be very different when viewed from this vantage point.

Relationships as Mirrors

> Our relationships are not separate from our spiritual evolution.
> Our relationships *are* our spiritual revolution.
> Your relationships have become your temples!
> Do you love enough to allow for the possibility
> of perfection in whatever life shows to you?
> – Greg Braden

My work with clients continues to show me how much the people in my life reflect back to me my own beliefs and behaviors. By seeing your relationships as a reflection of yourself, they teach you to see the part of yourself that may still need healing, or inspire you to greater expansion and growth. By holding the perspective that they are here to teach you what you need to learn about yourself, it is then that you allow them all the way into your heart. My clients have been a reflection of my own being, and the work I have done and continue to do.

They are me in some form or fashion, and when I hold them as my mirror, I allow myself to heal with them in their process. By the end of our engagement, we see the transformation and the creativity of their ability to mold themselves into a deeper connection with themselves, and all that is in their life – and it is pure joy. Just like our children, when they grow up, we see ourselves in them and how much our imprint is a piece of their being who they are. This is powerful. I want to share a poem that articulates this so well.

> The most visible creators I know of
> are those artists whose medium is life itself.
> The ones who express the inexpressible –
> without brush, hammer, clay or guitar.
> They neither paint or sculpt – their medium is being.
> Whatever their presence touches has increased life,
> They see and don't have to draw.
> They are the artists of being alive.
> – Unknown

Gavin has spent the last five years growing his video production company, which he started at age eighteen. He has already traveled all over the world, and made lots of amazing videos for brand names like Vogue, Victoria's Secret, Hefty, American Express, and more. He continues to stay focused on all he desires, and connected to what makes him come alive.

Gavin has taught me that not all who wander are lost. He wanders, and it belongs to him to wander. Wandering is part of the process of evolving. Give yourself permission to wander and not to know – this cultivates learning how to be with the unknown mystery of your life. I have no doubt that Gavin will create all that he desires. The reflection my children have shown me is my own wonder, joy, brilliance, insight, awareness and creativity. Their presence in my life has been and continues to be captivating. I continue to be in awe of their beauty, their intelligence and all of the mystery they remain open to.

Renee found a passion for training service dogs, and she is exceptional at it. She is married and happy, and she is trusting her Qoya and learning to love herself. Qoya was an ancient Incan tribe of women. The name Qoya translates in the Quechuan language as "Queen" – specifically, a feminine manifestation of higher consciousness as interpreted in Rochelle Schieck's book called *Qoya*. Renee reminds me of me when I was young. She is beautiful, smart, and she, too, has a quiet, magnetic presence. Renee reflects my own constant need to feel loved, and my deep spiritual quest – for she, too, is very empathic and aware.

My mom and I had wonderful conversations in our time together, and she always reflected my spiritual commitment to my own beloved. She has a deep sense of faith and trust in GOD, and spiritual practice with her divine guidance. I had a special connection with my father, maybe because I look like him, maybe because I was called "P.W.'s daughter" by many of his friends, maybe because he represented quiet power and strength. He was 6'4" tall and a leader in his field, and while he didn't lead through force, he led through the power of his presence and integrity.

Throughout my life, everyone has commented on how strong I am, and I owe that to my father's reflection. Both my parents were crucial mirrors for me in integrating my own masculine and feminine qualities in myself, and moving me towards a spirit-infused life. I know that life is turning out exactly as it is supposed to for each of us – and part of healing your heart is living in the understanding that you are exactly where you are supposed to be.

As I was writing this book, I asked myself, "Why am I in this writing workshop?" I realize it is helping some aspect of my healing; that is why. This is a process that heals, as is every experience in our lives. On the outside, it may look like it is about publishing a book, but if we choose to view it with an internal perspective, it is about healing some aspect of ourselves. I don't really know what words need to come out. The process is another step that supports me in living in the mystery of this life.

I am in the unknown. I think if it can help me to integrate more of what I am here to do, if it can help me live into more of my potential, then I have received what I came here for. The more of us there are, who share our voices and live our truths, the more that others can do the same. I see it as similar to "the hundredth monkey effect."

The hundredth monkey effect is a hypothetical phenomenon in which a new behavior or idea is claimed to spread rapidly, by unexplained means, from one group to all related groups, once a critical number of members of one group exhibit the new behavior or acknowledge the new idea.

The more we all take responsibility for deepening and healing our hearts, the more our friends, colleagues and children will do so also – and with the ripple effect of more people living an integrated, spirit-infused life, the more our ability as a whole will shift the consciousness of the planet from fear into love.

> Our relationships perfectly reflect our own inner
> process; they are wonderfully effective mirrors to help
> us see what exists in our own growth. So, if relationship
> difficulties persist, it is a message to us
> that a deeper level or our own healing is needed.
> – Shakti Gawain

How many times when my kids were growing up, did I ask myself, what are they reflecting for my own process? When

Gavin was mad, I would stop, take a breath and look at myself and ask, what is that anger reflecting for me? I took it in all the way and let the question work me, let myself sit with the question, and then responded to him. So often when we are angry, we deflect it to the other person or thing that made us angry, rather than taking responsibility for the feeling of anger. Gay Hendricks, psychologist and writer, says that arguing is vying for the victim position. That makes a lot of sense to me. And it makes you think twice about getting into an argument, considering the amount of wasted energy, as it accomplishes nothing productive.

If you can observe your relationships in your life and ask, "What are they reflecting for me?", when you are able to look inside yourself and sit with that reflection, then it creates a new strategy for how to respond to them – out of love and awareness – instead of anger, blame or whatever else your mind comes up with. Learning how to nurture and love them in the midst of nurturing and loving yourself creates a healthy awareness for all involved.

We so loved our community in HMB. When we moved, the kids and I sat in Meg's driveway, staring at the Pacific Ocean, and just cried our eyes out, all three of us. It was December of 2000. It was 7:30 AM on a beautiful morning, with the sun shining and the beautiful, blue ocean to greet us and wish us well on our way. We were beginning a new life in Texas, where my family of origin was waiting for us. We were scared, sad and nervous about driving into the unknown – and we were doing it all together.

During our ten-year transformation in HMB, we had experienced what it was like to be held in community and supported in our efforts, loved from the inside out. We will never forget that experience, for it made us who we are today. We took that moment, sitting in the driveway staring at the ocean, to honor our grief, our excitement and the gifts this amazing community had bestowed on us. Texas would offer us new growth, new friends and the safe haven of family.

"The secret to change is to focus all of your energy, not on fighting the old, but on building the new." – Socrates

The idea of moving to Austin, Texas from beautiful Half Moon Bay, California came after I had a conversation with my sister, Rachel. Rachel and I were the only mothers in our family of nine kids. There were seven girls and two boys, and only two of us girls, Rachel and I, had kids, along with both of my brothers.

We tended to talk a lot about being a mom, our challenges with our kids, and offering each other advice and support. We had been living in Montara, California, and Renee was not doing well at the middle school. She needed a better environment, and Gavin did also, at the elementary school. I could not afford to send them to the one private school on the coast, and to find a good school we would have to move to Palo Alto, which was over the hill and away from the coastal community we loved. I knew we couldn't afford that, or bear to leave the community we had built by the ocean.

In one phone conversation Rachel mentioned, "Why don't you move to Texas? You can help me with Daddy." My dad was having health issues, and we were not sure how long he would be with us. She said, "Move home – the kids can be with their cousins, and you will have family support and be with Daddy." I didn't know it then, but it would be the last eight months of his life.

I took it under serious consideration, and rather quickly made the decision that we move. It was December of 2000, right before the high-tech bubble burst in the Bay Area in March of 2001. Talk about perfect timing to leave. A part of me knew it was time to go, and I chose to listen to that small voice, despite my fearful thoughts. I chose to focus on how it would be good for us rather than on my fear of the unknown. My attention went to knowing that change would be good, and that we would be better for it, even though we did not know what we were getting ourselves into. Before we left, I told my employer I was moving. They offered to pay for a portion of my move, and to allow me to set up a virtual office in Austin and pursue clients for them in Texas.

It was all about being nimble, and building a new work environment. So, they had first hired me on my terms, with a nice salary that afforded me the ability to support my family – and now they were offering me the ability to work from Texas and pay for a portion of my move. This was a sign for me that I was listening to the right inner voice, and doing what was being asked of me next, even though I was not sure how it would turn out. We moved to Austin, and I set up a home office, and started integrating into the dynamic of my family of origin – and just being present with my dad.

I am so grateful for that time with him, although he was in an altered state most of the time, because there were moments when he was himself as I had known him. It's funny how our consciousness begins to change, as we approach death, Actually, it was no different than when the blinders came off after I moved out of the house in HMB. My perspective was changing, and I was able to be with my family and my father at a crucial time of all of our lives.

It was a miracle that I heeded the call and left when I did. The death of my father was the first physical death I had experienced in my life, and the first physical death my kids experienced. It was a profound healing experience for all of us. We struggled at first being in Austin, as we were transitioning into a new way of living in this new environment. It was so different. Nature was not a part of the life there, at least not in the way we had known it. Austin was a city with lots of concrete. We had lived on the Pacific Ocean, with beach and mountains as our playground.

I think when you live in an environment that incorporates the natural beauty of nature, it shifts you and changes how you live and think. All three of us were asking, "What are we doing here?" as we navigated our transition to living in Texas. Standing in line one day at a store, my daughter looked at me and said, "Everyone here is so nice." I said, "I know – it is so refreshing!" Towards the end of our time in California, we had noticed how stressed out people were, and angry. I have to wonder if this was actually the case, or our own reflection of California's no longer being congruent with where we were growing in ourselves.

It took a lot of emotional energy to live there. It was expensive, and for me, all the signs and feelings I had were telling me it was time to seek a different environment for myself and my family. The Texas motto is "The Friendship State." I've always believed that the people embody Southern hospitality, and it is such a great place to be from. I love that about my roots. To me, Texas-born people are authentic, friendly and gracious, and my kids were getting to experience that, while getting to know their family and roots – it was worth its weight in gold.

> "Progress is impossible without change, and those who cannot change their minds cannot change anything."
> – George Bernard Shaw

Renee enrolled in the public school, one of the top school districts in the city, and did very well. It was the right move for her. Gavin was immediately welcomed into the neighborhood group of boys, but struggled in school and in finding the right sport to be a part of. Everything was team-focused, and he is an independent soul. Renee struggled as well to find her sport, until we arrived in Austin and she was exposed to rowing. In a new environment with new relationships of family and new friends created new opportunities for myself and my children, that supported growth for all of us.

As you uncover the true reflection your relationships are mirroring to you, you begin to see the beliefs and thoughts that are asking for attention. In this new awareness, you realize which thoughts are serving your growth and which are not. From here, you can, first, change the beliefs and myths of the mind – and then, take the action that is best for you.

Myth Busting

"Emancipate yourselves from mental slavery, none but ourselves can free our mind." – Bob Marley

Let's talk about being accountable for your actions, thoughts, and beliefs. I was coaching a client the other night, Kayla, and she was up against the demons in her head. She had just started a new job that was a promotion, in the first healthy company she has ever worked for. Her boss, the Senior Vice President, was a wonderful man. She really liked him and looked up to him, and saw him as an amazing mentor. We discussed the negative thoughts she was having in her head, and how to allow that negative part of herself to be there and not push it away.

She calls this part of herself "scrappy" – kind of like the bully who won't admit that her feelings are hurt, and covers them up by being tough, as though it doesn't really bother her, but it does. I had no idea where the conversation was going; this is the part of coaching that is magical, when we are in deep exploration of a topic. I took her through a myth-busting exercise – which comes from the idea that all the beliefs in your head are myths, not truths, and you can bust the bad ones up and create new ones. Through the exercise, we busted the negative core belief she had about herself, that she was ineffective and never going to succeed. She believed that the negative voice was a character defect, and that it would always sabotage her. Her new belief, which she decided to trade it in for, was: I am patient, passionate, and powerful as an advisor serving the company in its transformation.

As we expanded the discussion, she came to the realization that this was about her owning the feminine qualities in herself. It's the part that doesn't have to be tough, but can acknowledge what she was truly feeling – and take action from there. Kayla is very athletic and has always gotten stuff done, but she leads from that masculine place inside herself. If you recall from the previous chapter, our masculine qualities are all about taking action. What she became aware of was that through the experience in this new role, and her awareness of how she wants to bring herself into this new position, she was going to have to start paying attention to her feminine qualities.

She needed to learn how to bring those qualities to the workplace, and how to communicate them in a professional tone. They are the part of her that acknowledges, feels and is present, direct, authentic, and patient with herself – and the part that is a woman who owns her truth. This doesn't mean she has to cry at the table – it is more about taking the opportunity to understand what her feminine presence looks like and feels like at work and with herself. Suddenly, her light bulb went off. We discussed ways in which to activate and pay attention to this aspect of herself, and ways to include her scrappy self at the same time. Remember, both qualities of masculine and feminine apply to both men and women.

As you become aware of all the aspects of yourself, it is important not to push away any of the voices in your head. It is more about including them, allowing them, and honoring them all. Through inclusion, and learning how to work with them in this context, you prevent them from controlling your thoughts, and those actions you desire to change.

This is self-love. It includes and allows, ease and flow into how you view all parts of yourself. It is not resistance and pushing. I like to describe it like this. Imagine a conference table where all the different voices of yourself are sitting around it. In Kayla's case, the scrappy voice was leading the meeting and sitting at the head of the table. But there was another part of Kayla that wanted to speak up. We will call this part of her Grace, the authentic leader within her.

By allowing "Scrappy" to take a seat, and activating Grace, Kayla is reframing her core belief. She is still acknowledging Scrappy, but no longer letting this part of herself lead the dialogue in her head. It is now Grace's turn to lead the conference. Scrappy is still at the table, and will continue to speak up now and then, but Grace is where Kayla's attention will be. Kayla will continue to recognize when Scrappy's comments show up, but she will see this with her new awareness, and make a choice to put her attention on Grace.

Notice that she will not beat herself up over Scrappy; she will simply recognize the voice, quietly thank it in her head, and focus on what Grace needs. This is learning to love all aspects of self.

This can be a hard concept to accept. Kayla came up with a strategy that she would begin to practice to start loving her "scrappy self," while allowing her passionate, powerful, patient feminine presence to drive her decisions. Now, you can bust your myths, too, with this simple exercise. Do this exercise now, and bust the beliefs that are not serving your growth, your purpose and your love.

Myth Busting Exercise:

Get out a piece of paper and draw a line down the middle of the paper. On one side, write out all the negative beliefs that go through your mind. On the opposite side, right out their exact opposite, the positive belief. Circle the ones that seem to be your core beliefs. Then answer the questions below.

- What is your myth? What is the belief you have, if any, that is playing in your life?
- Do you want to bust this myth?
- What are the costs and benefits of busting this myth?
- State the new myth you are replacing it with.
- Does it feel real for you?
- What is the #1 thing you can do on a consistent basis that would have the most impact in implementing this new myth?
- What touchstones/support do you need to remember to use it?
- Put the new myth in action and have fun doing it!

When I left my husband, and chose to support my two children, I was activating the masculine side of my own nature. I have always been overly responsible, always goal-driven, but I have learned to relax and allow myself to stop, nourish myself, and linger in the stillness of the journey. In doing so, I have become more present to who I truly am. This is why I love coaching so much. I went into coaching, not to help people, but to stop being so judgmental and to learn to hold myself in neutral. I knew that if I could master coaching a client, it would support my continued growth of deepening my love of self, and help me turn myself over to the guidance of the divine presence that resides inside me, instead of allowing my thoughts and neuroses to prevail. As a coach, you have to listen deeply to yourself, in order to listen deeply to your client. It is about partnering with your clients and holding them in their vision, until they can hold themselves there on their own.

It is about honoring their process, and going at their pace. Luckily, with my clients, I get to practice deep listening, being present and letting go of my ego every day. I wanted to learn to be the vehicle in my work and allow wisdom to move through me. Through the process of learning how to coach, I realized that I was doing what I was best at. I was playing to my strengths and being my best self, and I was getting the deep connection I desired in my life and in my work. I was able to honor the other and their individual process, and grow my own way of being. There is an immense satisfaction that I feel when partnering with clients to deepen their connection to self and all they desire to create.

I feel so grateful and fortunate to have been given the opportunity to coach others and help them to put attention on their inner world, and to support them in what they want to create. The gratitude I feel towards them is equal to the gratitude they feel towards me for allowing this partnership on their journey. I am consistently amazed at what they create, and the shifts they make inside themselves. It is true that whatever is happening outside of yourself is a reflection of what is going on inside yourself. I see it over and over again with clients. When they make internal changes in how they perceive, and where they place their attention, the external experience changes. To work with individuals and support them in opening their perspective from being outwardly focused to inwardly focused is a shift that supports happiness, health and presence of mind.

When you forge the dark shadows, and learn how to love all of you – when you are willing to stop, and allow emptiness, to not talk, to listen deeper and communicate more of who you are and what you desire – magic is the outcome. This is an exciting playground to work in, and it is a sacred journey I walk with all who work with me. To be able to be the keeper of their dreams is an honor.

Busting your myths and reprogramming your thoughts is like rebuilding your body. If you were rebuilding your body, you would commit to going to the gym and doing your exercises, and you would have reminders around to keep you moving in that direction, even when you did not want to. Using your touchstones helps to support you in staying committed to the new belief or behavior that you desire to create. I invite you to pick your touchstone, now that you have busted your old myth, and created a new thought pattern. What do you need to remind you to practice this new thought every time the old one appears? Pick your touchstone now.

The thoughts that worry you, I call them Tolerations, because they zap your energy and take up space in your mind. The thing about tolerations is that they never really go away; it is more about being aware of them and listening to what you need to change so as not to let them take up your energy and time. Texas allowed me to handle the tolerations that were front and center in my world in California: my kids' education and happiness, feeling supported with family close by and having the honor of being with my father for the last days of his life. Our move to Texas was one way of eliminating the tolerations that were occupying my mind, and opening myself to a new life that would bring new growth – and a whole new set of different tolerations.

Tolerations versus Acceptance

Coach U states that a toleration is something that is put up with or endured; it is a burden, and it eats up time, money, and mental space. Tolerations can be eliminated. Acceptance is understanding that while something may not be pleasant, it is a fact of that person's life, and as such, can become a positive factor with the right attitude and constructive planning for its presence. Often, the only difference between tolerations and acceptance is in attitude and approach. Acceptance implies that the condition or situation cannot be changed, except in the mind and future of the person.

By seeing the distinction between acceptance and tolerations, and eliminating any harmful and hindering tolerations, you begin to acknowledge and accept yourself and those around you. By removing and identifying the most paralyzing barriers, you open up your ability to acknowledge yourself. Humans have made tolerating an art form. We put up with, endure, take on, and are dragged down by people's behavior (including our own), situations, unmet needs, crossed boundaries, unfinished business, frustrations, and a myriad of problems.

Tolerations are certain obstacles to self-acknowledgment. Most tolerations can be eliminated, but they must be identified first. Even the tolerations that cannot be eliminated are easier to handle just by our awareness of them. Asking the right questions is important to getting to the real truth about how much you are tolerating, because you may be so accustomed to the tolerations that they have become your standard.

The following questions will help identify and, hopefully, eliminate tolerations:

- What are you putting up with?
- What have you been tolerating?
- What is bugging you that you wish wasn't?

- What is it costing you to tolerate this?
- What is the benefit of putting up with this?
- Why are you really doing this?
- Why do you want to stop tolerating this?
- How does having this toleration serve you? How would you be served if you didn't have this toleration?
- What is the new standard that will handle this and other tolerations?
- Who will you have to become to stop tolerating this?

Asking the right questions is important to getting to the real truth about how much you are tolerating, because you may be so accustomed to the tolerations that they have become the standard for you. Because they are energy zappers, they zap our bodies' ability to relax. Set a plan to handle one toleration at a time, and notice how you begin to have more energy and less stress in your life. This book was a major toleration for me… No joke, I have been putting this off for years. I have had people continue to tell me, "You need to write a book." My thinking kept me stuck in my tolerations. I kept thinking, "What do I know that the average person doesn't know?"

My realization in writing this book is that it doesn't matter what my fearful voice is saying, because it is about having my voice heard and, hopefully, support others in their process of honoring their truth. I finally got the message that there was no more time to tolerate this belief when I was on a yoga retreat in Tulum, Mexico, in March of 2016. The teacher asked us to have our soul speak to us. This is what my soul said to me: "Be like water and flow, and you will write the book. It is time to write your book." I knew when I got back that I needed to write, but didn't know how to start.

During my first week back in town, I came out of a yoga class, and happened to look at a flyer that stated: "Write your book in a weekend." It was advertising an Author Development

Program led by a man named Tom Bird. I read how he guides you into a meditative space, where you write from your right brain, not your left brain, and you create the outline of the book in one weekend. I was sold.

I signed up, and immediately felt a burst of excitement and energy. This is how it feels when you get a toleration handled – you get more energy. I was about to write a book by my own inner guidance, and I had finally decided to take action on it. My relationships were mirroring that it was time, and in spite of this, I continued to deny it for fear of, "How am I going to do this?" That was taking up my mental space and my energy, and it was not something I could delegate or delete. When you recognize your tolerations, you want to ask yourself: Can I delete it or delegate it – or do I need to do it?

If you can do one of these three, then you can get the toleration handled. Some tolerations you need to accept. Example: if your husband snores and you have no interest in getting a divorce, then you create a strategy for the snoring. He may sleep in the spare bedroom, or he goes to see a sleep specialist, or you delegate it to him to get handled in some other way because it is affecting your relationship. You accept the strategy necessary to make it work in your life, and you no longer allow it to be a toleration.

Part of being human is to learn how to manage the energy of your body, your mind and your soul, to care for yourself as a whole. This is living an integrated life. You begin to experience living a life full of reverence for yourself and all that is around you. You begin to live true to your values and who you are – and you find comfort in that, a confidence, in honoring your truth and your choices. This is powerful and life changing. It has been very transformative for me, and it has allowed my journey to transform into more pleasure than pain.

For years, I was the hippie. I did yoga and meditation, studied all kinds of esoteric topics, and experimented with things the average person doesn't even know about. When I had my kids, I brought them into the loop. I understand why John and I divorced: Part of the learning was to realize that I wanted to bring these kids up with the consciousness that came naturally for me. I could not do that as long as he was in the picture, with the drama and dysfunction he was experiencing. John made the choices that he needed to make as well, to stay true to his path. Now, after all these years, we are accepting of each other, supporting each other, and our kids get the best of both of us – along with the tools and consciousness of what I was asked to teach them as their mother. It was a duty of my journey to pass on these types of teachings to my lineage, and quite honestly, it was an honor and privilege to do this.

You know when you are on the right path, because what you seek finds you. We have all had the experience of being in the right spot at the right time. That happened multiple times in my life, especially when I decided it was time to reinvent myself and my career. And soon enough I found myself coaching. Luckily, I was aware and open enough to say YES.

This project of writing a book allows me to share the lessons I have learned in my own life as I uncover the process of creating the life I desire. This book is also a tool to continue to strengthen and build my brand as a coach, support my clients in their own work, and ignite my creativity to grow in ways I never expected.

You are here to share your potential with your colleagues, the teams you lead, your family and friends, and everyone you encounter. When you are fully engaged in the creation process of your life, you become magnetic – which attracts abundance, and feels really good.

I plugged into a force greater than me. I feel empowered, supported, and open to what shows up, and I feel so grateful to be given this time and space to practice, work, love, laugh, and support the shift of consciousness on the planet. This is the legacy I want to leave: that my being here mattered, and that I am leaving each person I know better than before we met.

I always had the vision that I would help people live authentic lives, congruent with who they are, because that is what I wanted so much for myself. This has been my personal journey, learning to live congruent to my truth. Every step along my path was necessary to teach me more about myself, and what I did and did not desire in my life.

I was good at recruiting, but there were parts I hated – the smiling and dialing and actual headhunting. However, the people I interacted with were pretty amazing, and the leaders I got to work with were pretty cool.

There was, however, a quality in them that felt asleep, and I wondered, if they were awake, how would they do it differently. I could see their blind spots back then, and how coaching could have helped in supporting these CEOs to be more effective. During one of my searches, I worked with a very successful firm to bring on some executives. The CEO wanted our firm, a neutral party, to interview all the partners and see where they stood in their growth, and the direction the company was headed.

One of the partners came clean with me while I was interviewing him; he talked about the dysfunction in the company and the leadership that was needed. He hated how political it all was, and I thought, how might coaching change them for the better. At the time, coaching was still a new concept in our business world. This process of interviewing the partners ignited the desire to dive deeper with clients and really serve them in their capacity to grow. When we have someone outside of us holding the space for us to process and bring our vision into creation, everything changes. We no longer have to hold it alone; we now have the power of two holding the same vision and intentions, and this creates momentum. This is how coaching supports the growth of a leader, a team, and an organization. When you become aware of all you are tolerating – and how much energy it takes to live with the toleration – you can then create a plan to get your energy back. In doing this, you move into acceptance, and this facilitates an open heart.

Chapter 3: Awakening Your Heart

To feel your heart is the key to happiness. This is where we feel and hear our truth. The heart holds more energy than the brain, and thus more power. If you can tap into the power of the heart – and heal any wounds that may show up there – by deeply listening to what it is saying to you and by putting your awareness into how it is directing you, then you will find true fulfillment based on your internal roadmap and not external influences. Let's explore the topics that are centered at your heart.

Courage

"You will never find peace of mind until you listen to your heart." – George Michael

Listen to the heart of the mother inside yourself, whether you are a man, woman, or child. It is time to take action in your own life for what you want and desire, and to realize you are a part of creating everything you are experiencing. You have a part of the creator in you. What you think, what you say, what you believe matters – and has an impact – even if you think it doesn't. I have example after example of how the divine speaks to me and has worked through me in my life. This is happening in your life as well.

This is what you have access to. All you have to do is change your attention, open your perspective, of what you give attention to, and start giving your attention to the inside instead of the outside, your heart instead of your head. To begin to use both sides of your brain to navigate your challenges and your work – and to start loving yourself more deeply.

I don't mean putting attention outside yourself by loving your spouse, partner or kids – we know how to do this – but to start learning what it means to love yourself. It starts with you. This is what I have noticed in my journey. By putting attention on my growth, on my internal process, on my healing and forgiveness, I help heal my family, my relationships, and my life – and I am able to overflow with even more love in all my relationships. This is so powerful, and we cannot squander our precious time here worrying about the neighbors and what they are doing. It is time to put attention on you, and what you need to clean up, heal, uncover, and explore.

It is important to focus on yourself as a living heart, and a major part of the process for this planet to heal. It is time to be accountable to your growth, passion, intelligence, emotions, and start operating in and expanding to the perspective of yourself. Some may say that this is a selfish approach. Selfishness refers to acting from the ego; but when you deal with the language of the heart and healing, it becomes selfless service, and it benefits the healing of everyone we interact with and, in turn, the planet. Once you begin to allow yourself to listen to your heart's guidance, then you begin to be conscious of the choices you are creating.

John is my ex-husband, and oh, how I love him. I always have, and yet our paths diverged. We came together to bring these two incredible souls into this world, and then it was time to separate. I had the foresight to keep him a part of our lives, even through some pretty tough times. I wanted the children to know who their father was, and it was never my intention to jump into another relationship.

My presence of mind was to allow parenting to work for me and to not complicate their lives any more than I already had. This is what worked best for me, and what I felt I was directed to do. Others are directed differently, and neither way is wrong or right. John disappeared out of our lives for one year after our divorce. He went to Texas to heal, and be with his chosen family, and recover.

When he came back, he saw the kids when he could – sometimes often, sometimes not. He was still navigating the next phase of his own healing and empowerment. When I decided to move to Texas, I hoped he would follow. I was still hoping we could get back together, that he would quit drinking, etc. I never stopped loving him, even though he was not helping support the kids and I was having a heck of time supporting them, on my own. He gave me money when he had it, but he was still struggling with his father and the lessons he was learning about himself from that relationship.

> "It takes courage to grow up and become who you really are." – e.e. cummings

When John was not interested in pursuing therapy, it prompted me to step into my courage, take action and surrender to the unknown of leaving him. I did it for my kids, to protect them, and little did I know I was doing it for my own empowerment, to survive and thrive and own my own power – and to get it back after having been taught to give it away in a co-dependent relationship. Little did I know that this was my first step in learning about what forgiveness was really about, and what its impact was on my own healing.

Forgiveness

"Forgiveness is the final form of love."
– Reinhold Niebuhr

    To live fully in your heart is to reclaim yourself over and over again throughout your life. It is to be alive, and living a spirit-infused life. No matter where you are or who you are with, you can experience life's magic and mystery by allowing yourself to dance with that mystery as it courses through and directs your life. In forgiving, you learn to forgive yourself; it is not about forgiving others. It is only when you truly forgive yourself that you can forgive another. It is not a head experience – it is a heart experience.

    It is an internal experience where you feel the love for yourself so deeply that no one can even describe it. Forgiveness is the core of so much resistance for us as humans. It is learning to forgive yourself, rather than beating yourself up or projecting onto others. Forgiving yourself when you feel you have done wrong is the first step to forgiving others. It is then that you heal your heart and dive into deeper love.

Yogi Bhajan, Kundalini Yoga Master writes:

    All healing is based on a relationship. The fundamental relationship is to your Self and to your Soul. You are missing nothing. You are complete within yourself. Whatever you have asked for is given. But we learn fear (or to fear ourselves).

    We learn that we are incomplete. We learn that we are flawed, bad, wrong, or ineffective. The fastest route to healing and to the experience of happiness is to forgive completely and limitlessly. Forgive, release, learn, love, and excel!

    What is there to forgive and release? The hundreds of inner tapes, patterns, and feelings that you have lived as if you are limited and inadequate. Regardless of the source of those patterns, they must be forgiven and released from the very neurons of the two hemispheres of the brain. Some of the most powerful and harmful feelings get distributed in the brain in such a way that we can talk about it forever without piercing the bodily sense of the emotion that forms its roots. Once we can connect to that area of the body and brain, it can be experienced and re-integrated with the rest of your body and mind. That wholeness is both the process and the result of healing.

Forgiveness is a powerful teacher, and one that John represented for me. He served me well in being who he was. He helped me own my power, strengthen my internal infrastructure and allowed me to love myself deeper. I don't know that I could have done that without him. What I judged in him is what I needed to own in myself. This was the greatest teacher. I thank him for loving me, having kids with me, and showing me what I was made of, showing me how strong I really am and how receptive and aware I am. He constantly made me see through his reflection, that it was time for me to reclaim life.

He supported me in this way through his own behavior, and I am eternally grateful for that. Through the healing I have done, I am able to see him and everyone else as my teacher, to help me forgive, love and trust deeper. He helped me move into acceptance of what is, and where I am, and what I am here to share. Without my family, I don't know where I would be. John, Renee, and Gavin have been three amazing mirrors to teach me who I am and what I am made of, and to love me through it all.

I could not have experienced myself in such a conscious way without them. They are my guides and my teachers, and I feel so grateful to have them in my life and to continue to receive their love. I was so scared, depressed, unsure of where I was going – and how I was going to make things work – during the years the kids were growing up. Through it, I developed strength and learning, how to be grounded, while staying connected and open and being willing to explore. And I continue to navigate uncharted territories with open awareness and love, and, hopefully, pay it forward to the next generation of beings who will lead us with their hearts.

It has been twenty years since my divorce from John. He moved to Texas, at the time we were moving from Texas to Colorado. Funny how life has a way of controlling the outcome of things. We were not meant to get back together, and we both know that now, but the miracle is that we have family holidays together. John has not remarried and neither have I, so we spend the holidays together with the kids.

We reunited as a family Christmas of 2014, our first Christmas together since the kids were little. We have healed and made our bond stronger ever since. John is now functioning, and supporting the kids with whatever they need – and for me, when I need anything, he is making up by always being there for me. It is an amazing thing to witness, such a miracle to be able to experience the true power of forgiveness.

We love each other from a much bigger place inside ourselves than we ever knew was possible. I believe that the result of our healing has to do with the fact that I have worked on healing myself, and John has healed his heart in his own way. I have chosen to put attention on the aspects of myself that I need to forgive, to love and to hold dear, and to nurture.

I have always been aware of the deep dialogue with my internal guidance systems, even though I have not always followed it. I feel proud about how I have lived my life and the choices I have made. At one point, my only regret was not letting my daughter go to the University of Denver (DU), allowing money be the factor, as it was a private school and cost $42K a year to attend at the time. Looking back, I'm not sure that was the right decision. I think fear took over me. She wanted to go there and I didn't even let the idea sink in. Renee had come back to Colorado from San Diego and didn't want to go back. She wanted to be closer to me and to home, but did not feel like Colorado was the place for her. Gavin and I were here, after we moved from Austin, TX, in her first year of college at San Diego State.

Had I let her go to DU, I believe her experience of Colorado would have been different, and it would have been the message to Renee that I trust that she knows what is best for her. In retrospect, it would have been a good school for her, as it was small, and filled with brilliant minds, like hers. I wish I had made it work, but I was tired, I was played the fear card and went into victim mode, not wanting the debt and not wanting to figure it out. I was clearly not open for having magic intervene to make it happen.

My resistance reared its head again. If we had made that choice who knows whether it would have been a more positive experience for her living in Colorado? While I regretted this decision, it created an opportunity for me to learn how to forgive myself. Learning to lean into my resistance gave me the next lesson of feeling where I needed to forgive. This broke down another concept I had been carrying around in my heart. And it supported me in reclaiming more of myself, and my ability to love myself and others. We are in a constant process of dying, rebirthing and reclaiming more of who we are as we heal our hearts.

Death, Rebirth and Reclamation

Death and Rebirth is a process that we go through over and over again in our lives and our work. The way I like to frame it is this: When you die (metaphorically speaking), you are dying to your old way of being in order to be reborn and begin anew.

You have to understand that you have the ability to renew yourself in ways you may not have imagined. We die multiple times throughout our lives to old beliefs, old desires, old addictions and old ways of being, processing, and seeing. In the dying, you are reborn. It is in practice of new behaviors and new routines that creates a rebirthing process and opens your awareness to a new way of being, a new perspective and an opportunity to grow your awareness and listen to your heart even more deeply.

Change is situational. Transition, on the other hand, is psychological. It is not those events, but rather the inner reorientation or self-redefinition that you have to go through in order to incorporate any of those changes into your life. Without a transition, a change is just a rearrangement of the furniture. Unless transition happens, the change won't work, because it doesn't 'take.'
– William Bridges, Author and Speaker

Some traditions call this "peeling back the onion." As we shed old beliefs and perceptions, we slowly grow into the core of who we are at the center of the heart, and bring that out more into our creative process of the lives we live. This "newness" can feel as though you are stepping into a portal in the new way you experience yourself, your life, and how you live your life. It is no different than the natural cycle of birth and death. It is all around you – in the plants, the animals and all aspects of life. The opportunity is to be aware of it in yourself.

By pausing and making the choice to be consciously aware that you are dying to your old beliefs and habits, you are able to honor the cycle of awareness and allow the rebirthing to occur in a more sacred, reverent way. It is these times of change that support us in pausing, reflecting and honoring the sacredness of the journey we are walking.

You may experience this through the loss of a job, the death of someone close, a divorce, or, in my case, the loss of my child's hearing (we will get back to that later) – any ending qualifies for this. These endings can be big or small. They don't all have to be major, life-changing events in our lives. Just as we shed our skin all the time, we are changing and evolving in every moment of every day. The point I want to make is to become aware of something bigger taking place within yourself, and to recognize it and honor the cycles of your evolution.

Through the process of death, we have to walk through grief. Learning to sit with grief as your teacher is powerful. I love this passage by Lynn Andrews, Author, Shaman and Teacher. I feel it describes the true teaching in grief:

GRIEF

Grief deepens you. It allows you to explore the perimeters of your soul. Grief is the only gateway to certain levels of consciousness, and it is a hard taskmaster. Through grief you can explore every aspect of your dark side – anger, pain, abandonment, terror, loneliness – these are aspects of the sacred wound that in our daily lives we usually try to ignore. Grief forces you to look at those parts of yourself that are not yet healed. If you can look at grief as a teaching, you will grow. The pain of grief is not the only teacher in this life, but if looked at properly, with awareness and an open heart, it is one of the greatest teachers of all. The seeds of wisdom and enlightenment are planted within the wounds of grief. What is lost can only come back to us again in higher ways.

When Renee lost her hearing at seventeen months of age, it was a call to transform how I had been living my life and the work I had been doing. After struggling through the pain and grief of the fact that my only child had lost her hearing just when she was beginning to talk, I had to reevaluate my values and my purpose. At the same time she lost her hearing, I had been offered the job I had been waiting for. I had to turn it down - I was now being asked to take a different path and teach my daughter to talk. This prompted our move out-of-state. At the same time, John was looking for work, and figuring out what his best career track would be. Our entire family structure was being shaken to the core to get out of the pattern we had been in and create something new.

This prompted our move from Texas to California to enroll Renee in an oral school for the deaf so she could learn to talk, with me as part of that process. I put my career on hold for the time being. Little did I know that I was in training to learn what it really means to communicate with oneself and others, as I learned how to teach my daughter to talk without hearing. Through this part of my journey, I slowly came back to myself. I reclaimed a part of myself that I had forgotten – and this part of my life ended up being a big part of what I do today, namely, to teach my clients about effective communication with themselves, in their work, with their careers and businesses.

Reclamation is important in your life's work. It is a process of remembering who you are at your heart, and learning to operate your life from there, instead of all the conditioning you have learned. You reclaim all the parts of yourself that you have pushed away in order to fit into the conditioning of our culture.

It is another step in acknowledging the love you have for yourself and your life. When you begin to reclaim your power, your beauty, your intelligence, your body, your thoughts, and your choices, this is what engages your genius. Just like the actual birth of a child, birthing yourself can be both painful and joyful, and it requires courage, patience and trust. Following your heart and activating your intelligence will support you in reclaiming all of who you are, and move you towards living an integrated life – full of heart, and grounded in this world, yet connected to the mystery.

This is the place of peace that we all seek. It has been my experience that one of the most powerful tools that has supported me in my own healing and reclamation has been accepting the belief that everything is here to teach me something about myself and my process of growth. I feel that the key component is being consistent, and committed to living a life where everything serves your growth.

Let's explore your commitment and how it is the driver of your life. It is important to know what you are truly committed to, and to be aware of where you ignore commitment – and where there are opportunities to strengthen it.

Commitment

"Commitment is what transforms a promise into a reality." – Abraham Lincoln

One of my friends came to the conclusion that a spiritual practice she was very interested in was fake, based on something she read on the internet, not on what she had been experiencing or feeling. She decided she was no longer going to believe in it. I find that interesting. So, where do we allow our head to take over and the fear rule? Where do we tend to not believe in what we feel? If the idea is only in our heads, this is the key. It is the feelings in our hearts that we must pay attention to.

In order to have more magic in your life, you have to make the commitment to allow yourself to be open to receiving it. You have to shift your perception and awareness so as to notice the magic in the simplest of activities, from witnessing a magnificent sunrise to the amazing wonder of a child. Magic supports you to live in the present moment.

My experience of magic is that it stops you in your tracks when it shows up. It gets you out of your head, and for a split second, you feel connected to something so much bigger than yourself. It makes you stop, pause, and take notice. You can have these experiences all the time if you choose. Let's address what stops you from experiencing even more magical moments in your life. Sometimes a person who doesn't see magic in their life doesn't need to at that point, but if this is speaking to you, just maybe there is something in you that wants more magic than what you are currently experiencing.

Perhaps you hold the belief that magic is something that doesn't require your participation. In order to stop looking outside yourself for miracles, you have to come to the realization that you are a co-creator in attracting any miracles in your day. If we choose to believe that we create everything in our life, then that includes the magic as well. This requires that you make the choice to put your time and resources on yourself – into your own commitment to yourself – with a practice that keeps you focused on your internal healing. Shifting our internal reality takes commitment and time to focus on our internal beliefs, feelings and thoughts, and how those shape our behaviors. Doing this is what creates deep internal fulfillment and, curiously enough, more miracles than you can imagine.

My commitment to this awareness practice came through Kundalini Yoga. I remember how much it opened and cleared a path for me, how much stronger my attention grew to listening to my inner voice and how much more attention I chose to put on that voice and the space inside myself. That is what Kundalini yoga does: it supports you in uncovering yourself, like peeling back an onion – as previously discussed. This practice has taught me how to ground myself, and eliminate my attachment to the personal – and in some amazing way, to remove the neurosis from my subconscious. What I have experienced as a result of this practice over the last twenty-five years is that I now recognize how much we are all alike, how much we are all suffering, how much we all want Peace, happiness and fulfillment – and that it is actually attainable. But we have to be accountable to a practice that awakens this, and be a willing participant in it.

When you are committed to awakening yourself through a practice you do every day, even when you don't want to do it, you begin to train the mind to be a slave to you, rather than having you be a slave to the mind. This allows you to see when and what you are resisting, and when you get caught in your patterns of dysfunction that support your head instead of your heart. Whatever your practice is, whatever your intention, ask yourself what your level of commitment with it is.

What we are doing here is putting new software into our brain, and cleaning out the subconscious. This is no easy task, as we have been programmed from the time we came out of the womb. So, commitment is a big deal, and it is a daily activity to create the depth of change that we wish.

If you have a practice, I congratulate you. Keep it up. If you have a practice that you undertake once a week, and it allows you to be able to expand your awareness with what is in your heart – and observe yourself in a mindful way – I invite you to step it up to more than one day a week. This level of work takes daily attention. Meditation is like a shower for the mind. You take a shower every day to clean your body. It is no different with meditation. You have to clean your mind every day to keep healthy and free from unwanted thoughts.

This is so important, and, at first, it seems so hard to do. This is why I am writing this book: to help you shift your thinking, your perspective, in how you choose to care for your soul. I would love for a community to grow out of this, in which individuals support each other in this way.

As you learn to integrate all these aspects of yourself, you begin to live a multi-dimensional life. You listen more deeply – seeing more than just what you see with your eyes, and you trust your inner knowing. Being able to hold appropriate boundaries, leaning into any resistance and allowing yourself to merge all three of these aspects of yourself: body, mind and heart. When all three of these qualities integrate into one form, you can experience what Ken Wilbur calls an "integral life." Ken Wilbur is an American writer on transpersonal psychology, who has created his own Integral Theory, a four-quadrant grid which illustrates how to synthesize all human knowledge and experience.

Wilber explains the need for an Integral Approach in the following way: In our current post-modern world, we possess an abundance of methodologies and practices belonging to a multitude of fields and knowledge traditions. What is utterly lacking, however, is a coherent organization, and coordination, of all these various practices, as well as their respective data sets. What is needed is an approach that helps to enrich and deepen every aspect of our lives through an understanding of exactly how and where each one fits in relation to all the others. Through the Integral approach, we reveal the previously unseen possibilities for a better, more compassionate, and more sustainable future for all of us.

Imagine a world where we live from this place, in total Inclusion of each other. To create this experience, we have to start by strengthening our emotional intelligence. Emotional Intelligence is defined as the ability to identify your own and others feelings so you can interpret and manage them effectively. By making a commitment to observe how you are feeling at any given moment, promotes the experience of being present with yourself and others. I can only speak from my experience, and I don't feel this way all the time – but I do, more often than not. My experience is a feeling of being very grounded in my body and connected to my heart, aware of what I am feeling inside me as well as having a very strong intuitive knowing. Think of your body as being a column of light between heaven and earth, but with roots that are deeply grounded in the earth. This visual helps me. We can bring heaven here on earth by using our bodies to connect with the divine in our hearts, and thus become instruments of the divine. Through my practice, I feel myself being calmer than hurried; I am confident more often than insecure; and I trust a lot more when being in unknown territory. This is a place of much less stress, much less trying to figure things out – and being in the flow where solutions come effortlessly and easily. And the feeling fills me with light, joy and connectedness. Here are some simple steps to start with to begin a practice of awareness and strengthen your own emotional intelligence.

- Think about what practice helps you get out of your head and creates a space of calm.
- How often, realistically, can you start practicing every week?
- If you already have a practice, GREAT! How can you step it up a notch?
- When would you do it in your day?
- What may sabotage you from practicing?
- What support do you need to put in place to be aware of where you sabotage yourself, so that you won't?
- Begin your practice.

With this slight adjustment, you begin to grow your commitment to living a conscious path with yourself, your family, your colleagues and your work.

Perception is defined as "the state of being or process of becoming aware of something through our senses." When you get committed to working with your perception, it shifts, and opens your awareness, and allows for more illusions to drop, more awareness to be had, and more of your truth to be revealed. There is a softening that happens, a deepening in the inner being from the inside out. I see this often with clients, and it is amazing to witness how a subtle shift in their commitment to their own growth begins to shift their life in the direction they desire. I love this statement about the depth of commitment by Author, Oriah Mountain Dreamer, in her book, *The Invitation:*

"I want to know if you have been through a night of despair, weary and bruised to the bone, and still know how to get up and do what needs to be done to feed the children."

This is the level of commitment required for deep, sustainable growth from the inside out. There are many different venues for self-growth. The first step is asking the question: Where are your edges for growth in your life, and are you currently pushing those edges? If not, what would it look like if you were?

One of the clients I am coaching, Janice, has decided to go to coaching school. She just enrolled in her classes, and she said that it is so hard, because it is all about working on yourself first. It is about looking inside, instead of outside. It is about deep thought and feelings and contemplation.

I feel that, in my life, commitment came or was amplified when I had kids; but even before that I was always exploring new options and places I could take myself. I was always willing to try something new and different. I enrolled in a personal foundation course in the early '90s, called Temenos (this company is no longer operating under this name) when I lived in the Bay Area. It took my awareness to the next level. I look at what I learned there, and there was so much.

This was a personal foundation group, based in Mill Valley, and the work we did there was so amazing. I also enrolled my sister, Meg, who lived in the area. It was amazing to have her be a part of something so deep, and for us to support each other through our growth. I know it helped Meg, and it helped us in our commitment to doing the deep soul work, while supporting each other, and in being accountable to the program we were in. It helps to have friends, a coach, a therapist, someone in your life who is speaking the same language, for it is hard to explore unknown internal territory on your own. It is too easy to get distracted by your mind, and there is too much room for self-sabotage. On top of that, a buddy can offer a perspective that you may not see. They can open a door to awareness by sharing their experiences of you – and this helps open our blind spots. Having a buddy helps create accountability to keep going, when the mind wants to bail out. With any commitment we make, it is more motivating and easier to keep going through the rough patches, when you have others doing the same who can offer support.

Our children are always great reflections for us. When I look at Gavin, I see his ability to manifest, his driven actions around his work, and his humor. I love his humor. It makes me feel so light and happy, and it teaches me to take myself lightly. It was my children who spurred me to have a commitment to a practice – and thank God for that. I am not sure I would have come through it as honest, and so tuned into my truth, had I not been committed to my spiritual practice.

I knew I was supposed to be taking care of the kids without John's influence. It was a way for me to share with the kids the practices that would shape their lives for the better, and to learn how to process the emotional challenges they were experiencing. Because I was healing, and learning how to live in my own truth, I was able to teach them through my actions. As the saying goes, when you want to master something, teach it. I had plenty of opportunities to do this. I made the choice to raise them in an environment where ritual, yoga and reverence were front and center, and to expose them to all the teachings and experiences that were shaping me. As a result, we continue to heal and transform together.

The key in cultivating commitment is not to beat yourself up. There will be days when you miss your practice, and the great thing is that we can begin again the next day. Trust your own process. Sometimes the work I do, such as writing this book, is so deep that I need a break. There are pages that force me to go deep and become emotional, and then we need a break – a lighter conversation – before we dive back into the deeper conversations and thoughts to digest. Making decisions based on our commitment to what we believe is important to staying present.

Being able to stay present with yourself ensures that when you are caught off-guard, you are able to act on the new pattern you have been practicing that represents your truth. This is how you notice that your pattern is shifting. Here is one such moment for me with my son Gavin.

When Gavin was a senior in high school, and he had been enrolled to go to college, he came into my office and said, "Mom, if I go to college, I am going to waste your money." I sat there, stunned, reacting inside my head, thinking, "Oh my God, he has to go to college. What will he do? How will I continue to support him?" A myriad of questions ran through my mind in a split second. But in that split second, I took a breath and reflected on Gavin as a mirror for my own growth – and thank God I did, because it was a significant reflection into who I really am as a spiritual being.

I asked him, "What are you going to do?" He said, "I want to build my video business." In tenth grade he had taken a video/camera course, and he fell in love with the art form. He was exposed to it a little through my sister, Meg, who has a passion and hobby for photography. I said, "Okay, but you'll have to let me coach you." He said that was okay. We began building goals around this idea, including actions he would take. What is important to point out is, in that moment, when Gavin opened my office door and said I will waste your money if I go to college, I stopped and thought, "If I tell him he has to go to college, I will undo the last eighteen years of teaching him to trust himself and his intuition."

I didn't want to do that, so I said okay. It was another magic moment for me in my healing journey that I will never forget. It was one that I am proud of, and one that validated my commitment to my work of self-love for both Gavin and myself. Because of the level of commitment to doing my own inner work, and the practice I had created daily, I was able to shift in that split second from all the fearful thoughts that were going on in my head, and take a breath, and ask myself, "What can I learn in this moment?"

There are so many ways in which we are not accountable to ourselves and to others. It all starts with being accountable to your own growth, and being accountable to your heart, mind, and body. It is this triad you must pay attention to, and learn how to shift the thinking – how to balance the brain, focus the mind on what supports you, then reach into the body and ask, "What do you need to feel energized and alive?" We can look at the body, mind and heart as the holy trinity, the sacred chamber, and put attention on the area that gives the most support first – and then, navigate from there and trust your instinct. It is important to remember that your commitment to reprograming your beliefs and thoughts are the first step to taking action on that which you desire in your life. Once you make the commitment, you will be shown the tools you need to bust the beliefs and myths of the mind and take the action that is best for you.

Take time to tear down the beliefs and myths that do not serve your growth, and replace them with what you want to experience in your life and your work. It is time to be mindful that you are a co-creator while you are here, and to be present to every breath, every thought, every reaction – and to start being intentional in the choices you make. Part of loving yourself is learning to commit to yourself in all different kinds of ways: the way you hold boundaries, the way you listen to yourself, the way you take care of yourself, the words you choose to speak and the judgments you make.

When you begin to acknowledge all parts of yourself and your life, you begin to spread that acknowledgment to others in your life. Take a moment, right now, and spread a little love balm on yourself.

Exercise:

- Make a list of ten things you want to acknowledge yourself for.
- Now do a happy dance in honor of YOU.
- Take a deep breath in, close your eyes, and bow to the power of how great acknowledging yourself makes you feel.

Acknowledgment – The Love Balm

"Acknowledgment is the only way to keep love alive."
– Barry Long

Self-hatred and beating ourselves up is not necessary – it is a learned pattern. Let's talk about the next time you go into beat-up mode, and what a supportive dialogue with yourself would sound like. Think acknowledgment. Spread love on your thoughts. Acknowledgments are love balm. Think about when you compliment someone, or receive a compliment – it always feels good.

Giving compliments makes both the receiver and the giver feel good. It is a way of saying that you matter – you count – and I see you. It is such a magic strategy to use on everyone, but especially yourself. If you can harness this within yourself, you can expand this into all the relationships in your life and work, and transform anything bad into something good. We live under the programming of negative thinking, negative media, all kinds of focus on what is not working.

Where you put your attention grows. If you focus on the negative, that will grow; if you focus on the positive, then that will grow. Focus on the positive, and it's possible to experience the magic – and you stop the habitual pattern of doubting yourself and beating yourself up. Negative self-talk is a sabotage tool; it is how you manipulate yourself – it keeps you in victim mode and prevents you from reclaiming the amazing being that you are.

Negative self-talk breeds more negativity in your life, and it is not productive. In yogic technology, we have a positive mind and a negative mind, and they both serve us. The negative mind serves us in letting us know when we are in danger, but when it is out of balance, we become overwhelmed with negative thinking. This indicates that fear is running the show. If you are experiencing a lot of negativity, use the negative as opportunities to shift into positive thought. Use them as a reminder to practice. It reminds you that you have a choice in how you chose to care for yourself in that moment. I can beat myself up, or I can love myself based on the thoughts I am thinking and the words I am saying. Take the opportunity to send loving kindness to yourself. If you haven't tried the myth-busting exercise, go back to chapter 2 and try it now.

Do something that gives you joy, makes you laugh or gives you pleasure. I call these types of practices daily delights. I invite you to create your daily delight list, which consists of ten to twelve items that give you delight, joy and pleasure. Post it where you can see it every day, and do at least one of them a day – as a way to spread your love, and honor your unique being. The more love you spread on yourself, the more positivity and abundance comes into your life.

If you want positive experiences in your life, then direct your mind to what is working every day and celebrate that. Grow the love inside of you so that your relationships begin reflecting that love back to you.

How often do you allow yourself to be really present, and in a state of wonder and awe? We see this all the time in little children. We all love this experience when we have it. I feel closer to something that is magical and awe - inspiring when I am in this state. It takes me out of this realm of reality into a whole other dimension, into a way of thinking that is positive, where I lose track of time and space, and am totally one with the experience. This is how I want to live my life.

It is not for us to figure out the how or the why, or to hold expectations. It is for us to dream and follow our hunches and take action on what brings us joy and pleasure, and then the way will be made clear. Caroline Myss is a five-time *New York Times* bestselling author and internationally renowned speaker in the fields of human consciousness, spirituality and mysticism, health, energy medicine, and the science of medical intuition. In her book, *Advanced Energy Anatomy,* she offers three things that help us humans stay in the present moment:

- Make no judgment.
- Have no expectations.
- Give up the reason to know why something is the way it is.

In my opinion, this is a lifetime practice.

Gratitude is a wonderful practice for spreading love balm. It creates those times when things just line up, and everything is happening that you desire – effortlessly. This is being in the flow of magic, and it allows for miracles to abound. My life is full of miracles, and I experience them over and over again. Renee lost her hearing when she contracted meningitis at seventeen months of age. It was a miracle that we were able to get her the cochlear implant; it was a miracle that John found the Jean Weingarten Peninsula Oral School for the Deaf (JWPOSD), and that we were able to teach her to talk. It was a miracle that we survived the divorce, and that I figured out how to raise two kids on my own, and that John and I have forgiven each other. It was a miracle that we had such a sacred community to help us during the darkest times of my life. It was a miracle that I found Kundalini yoga. It was a miracle that I knew I would have one boy and one girl, and I did. So many miracles.

I want to be present to more miracles, and present to more awareness. I want to keep expanding my awareness until I die, to be accountable for uncovering the magic and the gratitude. Gratitude can shift a life. I am currently in my life doing 26 days of writing out ten gratitudes a day, and reading them out loud. I pay attention to it every day, and experience this feeling even deeper in my heart.

I always declare ten gratitudes in the morning and right before I go to sleep, but now I am writing them out and saying them out loud, and it is transforming me. It expands the heart, and even changes the brain chemistry. According to a New York Magazine blog entitled "Gratitude: How Expressing Gratitude Might Change Your Brain" by Christian Jarrett, Studies are showing the positive impact that gratitude has on our brains.

Time and again, studies have shown that performing simple gratitude exercises, like keeping a gratitude diary or writing letters of thanks, can bring a range of benefits, such as feelings of increased well-being and reduced depression, that often linger well after the exercises are finished. Now a brain-scanning study in NeuroImage brings us a little closer to understanding why these exercises have these effects. The results suggest that even months after a simple, short gratitude-writing task, people's brains are still wired to feel extra thankful. The implication is that gratitude tasks work, at least in part, because they have a self-perpetuating nature: the more you practice gratitude, the more attuned you are to it, and the more you can enjoy its psychological benefits.

These practices I mention here in this book are only tools to support you in living well and being fully alive. They help to support you in living from a place of love – then you can leave a legacy that makes a positive impact on your family and friends, and helps our planet heal.

The heart is a hundred times more powerful in its electromagnetic field than the mind. Focusing only on the desires in your heart, and how to live them in your life, will have a very big, positive ripple effect that impacts beyond your life to future generations.

Leaving a Legacy

"Please think about your legacy, because you are writing it every day." – Gary Vaynerchuk

I want to leave a legacy of empowerment and willingness to chart into unknown territory around our feelings and emotions, and growing our emotional intelligence. I want to support others who are starving for this kind of stimulation, who are heeding the call of their own inner voice. I know so many of you are, and I want to be there to support you, honor your process, share the love with you, work with you in gaining your power and opening your awareness.

I want to be here to teach you how to hold the container of love for yourself and others when it is tough and challenging. I want to leave a legacy of living an integrated life, one in which both my heart and my head are felt, listened to and integrated. One in which I listen to the still, small voice inside me with an open heart, to live connected to my inner knowing. I want to trust that I know the unknown. I want to leave a legacy for my children, and their children, of awareness and adventures in self-discovery – and yet still be a part of this world. To let my presence make a positive impact while I am here, and to allow my presence to drive others to explore their edges, their depths, their darkness and their delight.

I want to revel in my delight, my fun and my pleasure. Mama Gina is another great teacher I have had the benefit of studying with. She taught me to embody that the power of a woman is loving her pleasure and making sure she pleasures herself often in whatever way works for her. Pleasure and joy are the key to a happy life. The key to living in your joy and pleasure is dealing with the distractions and the places inside and outside of us that move us into thinking we don't deserve joy and pleasure.

By listening to your inner voice, you are listening to yourself and growing trust to experience more pleasure and joy in your life. Loving yourself allows you to look at the children of your world and realize that they are here to teach you. You are their guardians while they are here. But in truth, they are your reflection, and they are here to help you grow more fully into your potential. I think you can ask any parent, and they will agree that having children forces you to grow in areas you don't always choose. Some of the ways they are here to teach you are to wonder, to play, and to help you experience pleasure and delight by simply being.

Our spiritual practice every week as a family was to practice yoga and meditation together. One day when Renee was a senior in high school, and I was walking past her bedroom, she said, "I don't have to practice yoga anymore." I said, "Fine. It is in your tool bag; you have it if you need it." Gavin and I continued practicing that year. She joined occasionally.

One year later, her first year in college, she was on the junior varsity rowing team. She had made the Dean's List and was incredibly stressed. She called me and asked, "What meditation should I do? I am so stressed out." She continues to this day to practice yoga and meditation on a regular basis, as well as utilize other tools and strategies that we share with each other. Gavin has stayed very connected to his body – always stretching it, biking, and continuing to listen to his inner voice.

It is so much fun having kids who are multi-dimensional in how they live and how they view the world. They are amazing teachers and reflections for me, and it is so fulfilling to see them grow up loving themselves and making smart choices for their lives. I am so proud of them – and so proud of me for surviving it and sticking to my guns and my commitment to raise consciously-inspired kids with heart. The practices I chose to put in place, which they learned at a young age, have instilled in them the ability to trust their intuition, acknowledge and love themselves, and always create space for not doing anything.

They are so much more aware than I am, and they trust themselves so much more. It is amazing what conditioning does – both productive and unproductive.

By putting growth as your focus, you then begin to awaken your consciousness to the choices you make. And you begin to live a spirit-infused life that embodies behaviors that reflect how you want to be, communicate and show up in the world.

Choices

I have come to the frightening conclusion
That I am the decisive element.
It is my personal approach that creates the climate.
It is my daily mood that makes the weather.
I possess tremendous power to make life miserable or joyous.
I can be a tool of torture or an instrument of inspiration;
I can humiliate or humor, hurt or heal.
In all situations, it is my response that decides
Whether a crisis is escalated or de-escalated,
And a person humanized or de-humanized.
If we treat people as they are, we make them worse.
If we treat people as they ought to be,
We help them become what they are capable of becoming.
 – Johann Wolfgang von Goethe (1749-1832)

If you can't make the choice to change your own sabotaging behavior for yourself, then start by doing it for your kids. If you don't have kids, do it for the next generation. They want us to wake up; they want to keep learning from us. We have so much wisdom to share, so much to pass on. How enriched our world would be if each of you were accountable to growing your Emotional Intelligence.

Think about the changes that could be made, if your attention were focused on the aspects of yourself that are happy and full, rather than what is not working, what you worry about and what you fear. To linger in the magnificence of who you are, and to own and honor this in yourself and others – this is what will change generations and the world. This is what will make life here on Planet Earth a better place. The solution's inside of us, not outside of us. Shift your thinking from outside yourself to inside – to your heart, to how you feel, and to what your sensations are.

Start observing and notice what you feel, and what you experience. This awakens awareness and expands emotional intelligence. Part of being in human form is learning how to manage and care for the energy in your body, your mind, and your heart – to care for yourself, and all the aspects of yourself. When you do, you can live a life full of reverence for yourself and all that is around you.

When you begin living in this state of awareness, and in a constant state of growth, you begin to live true to your values and who you are. You find comfort and confidence in honoring your truth and your choices. This is powerful. I feel so empowered by my choices that now, when I feel disempowered, it is so strong that I take note, and I have to act on it immediately by changing what I am thinking or doing to something that is more productive.

I had the great fortune of studying with Stephen Aizenstat, at the Pacifica Graduate Institute. He had a dream-tending course in Montecito, California. It was a six-month course, where I could learn to tend my dreams. I loved the idea of studying with him, so I decided to apply for the scholarship. I was living in Austin at the time, and I figured that if I get it, I am supposed to go. I got the scholarship and off I went to Santa Barbara, once a month for five months, to learn how to tend my dreams.

Some African tribes believe in the power of tending dreams, and that the dreams we have are messages from the spirit world. They believe it is important to tend them and listen to their messages, as this will help us stay in our heart and direct our lives towards our potential. Stephen studied with these tribes and brought this work to the United States in his work at Pacifica Graduate Institute. In these African tribes, the women who tend the dreams, are called Dream Tenders. They are usually elderly women who help their family and villages.

Our class, which consisted of thirty people, gathered in Montecito, near Santa Barbara. We tended our dreams every month. One of the men in the group was from Colorado. I happened to have a dream about moving to Colorado, and we tended it in the group. My action from the dream was to explore the Denver area and see where it led me. In this methodology of tending dreams, it is important that once you tend the dream, you take an action or direct attention to the topic that the dream is pointing towards. directing you towards.

For one holiday vacation, I had decided to take the kids up to Colorado to ski. While we were there, Gavin said to me, "I could live here." Then I had the dream, worked it in my dream-tending class and got clear messages to begin planning our move to Colorado. Gavin and I made our list of what we wanted in a house, and I started searching for jobs. One weekend, my sister Meredith was visiting Austin and brought a map of Colorado, and we discussed where I would live.

I needed to live close to her. She is married with no kids, and I wanted her to be near, in case I needed help with watching Gavin. She lived in Evergreen, and I knew I wouldn't live there, as I would probably take a job in Denver and needed a shorter commute. I asked her about Golden. She said that would be a good spot.

I came home that day after my discussion with Meredith, and when I walked in the door, Gavin said, "Mom, I figured out where we should live." He had pulled out the map of Denver and said, "What about Golden?" One more confirmation for what I knew I had to pay attention to. We flew up, and spent a three-day weekend in Golden. I had three interviews, and I knew I would be given an offer. We looked at lots of homes for rent, and decided that the very first one we looked at was the one we liked the most.

It was over my budget, so I decided to call the landlord, and talked them down $200. The landlord was a School of Mines professor, a young man, and he'd had school kids renting his home prior. He wanted a stable family as renters instead. He dropped the price for us and we rented the home. We were so excited. We loved the neighborhood and its proximity to hiking and biking trails, right out our front door. It was similar to Half Moon Bay, with nature in easy access.

After we rented the home for one year, the landlord wanted to raise the rent by $400.00. I told him that I should just go buy a home instead, and he said, "Make me an offer." I did - we bought the house the following year. Never in a million years did I think I would be here, living in the mountains, in this nice home that I now own. But I wanted to stop moving with the kids, and I wanted to get grounded and stable, for myself and for Gavin for the rest of his school years. We had been moving since I left John – and it was time to stay in one place and own a home.

After the purchase of our home, I was going through old files one day and found the list that Gavin and I had made of what we wanted in a home for our move to Colorado. This was the list we compiled when we were living in Austin. We made the choice that we would meditate together on this list, and talk about it, and vision it into our life. When I read the list, I was once again in awe of miracles that abound in our lives. We had created a home with all the things on the list, except a cat door, added later. Our ritual of creating the list, and putting our attention on it, created a shift in our thoughts and beliefs – thus creating the home we desired, and we were, once again, in complete awe of what we created.

Magic continues to abound when we choose to make conscious choices, and to create rituals and accountability practices around those choices. This is what creates the energy to manifest and move towards what we desire.

Rochelle Schieck, Author of Qoya beautifully describes ritual in this passage.

Ritual is a way to merge the traditions of the past with where we live in the present, to make an investment in our future. In a modern lifestyle of constant movement, learning about ritual is a way to press the pause button to honor, celebrate, grieve and dance with the various moments of our lives. Ritual invites us to step out of the momentum tunnel of going through the motions and, consciously, take time in our day to sit with the sacred and anchor our hearts in gratitude, be open to insight and inspiration as we dare to dream bigger dreams.

Rituals, Intention and Living with Reverence

Reverence is defined as deep respect for someone or something. Living a spirit-infused life requires the practice of reverence. For me, cultivating reverence comes through the rituals we create in our lives, through our beliefs and our behaviors. We had an exercise at dinnertime when the kids were growing up called "the rose and thorn." when the kids were growing up at dinnertime called "the rose and thorn." One day when Gavin was in third or fourth grade, he came home from school and said, "Mom did you know that dinner time is the time when the family comes together and talks about their day, and that all families do this, not just us?"

It was a new concept to him that we were not the only family that had this ritual. My guess was that in his mind, it was some sign that we were normal. He had viewed us as out of the norm with our yoga, chanting, and the other rituals we practiced. Rituals that seemed normal in California seemed out of the box, once we moved to Texas and made him feel his difference. It was so amazing to hear him say that. I said, "Yes, our ritual at dinner time is what most families do – they just may do it in their own way."

When my children were growing up, we had candles every night at dinner. I always felt that candles made things more sacred, and that was the energy I wanted for our mealtime. Since my divorce, I decided that we would use the good china every day, and we did. The start of dinner time consisted of our ritual, the "rose and thorn" exercise. What was the rose of your day? What was the thorn of your day?

This allowed each of us to feel the other's thorn, or pain, and it gave all of us the opportunity to learn what it was teaching – not only the person who was speaking about it, but all of us at the table. It was my way of teaching my kids, in that moment, how everything serves our growth – and the importance of learning that through our dinner dialogue, and daily awarenesses, a sense of reverence for life grew in each of us. We still do this on occasion when we are together, and it is always interesting to hear what they have to say even though they are adults now. I even do it at dinner parties, and it opens up a field of honesty and vulnerability that connects us all.

Another weekly ritual was our spirituality practice as a family. When the kids were young, I told them they had to have spirituality in their lives. I decided to give them a choice one day, because they always complained about going to church. I said it was church, or yoga and meditation, every week. They could pick, but it had to be one of those, to insure spirituality in their lives. We visited several different churches, but they grew up with yoga and meditation in their environment since they were born. That was their preference, and so we started weekly classes in our living room every Sunday evening.

It was our Sunday ritual to begin the week. This was a sacred time of teaching them how to work with their thoughts and their bodies to listen to their hearts and grow their intuition. And it took accountability on my part and commitment, even when I did not want to teach it. But I am so glad I did.

The rituals I chose to raise them with, and that they had a choice in as well, allowed us as a family to experience vulnerability, intimacy and reverence for the lives we were living. Rituals infuse a life of spirit and intention into our environment. They impact how you choose to believe and behave and behold the sacred throughout your life, and this brings the realization of how precious your time is here.

Chapter 4: My Life as a Gift

I am committed to being engaged with life, and to being continually open to expanding my awareness, so that I can support others to live happier and more engaged lives. I am here to help you realize that your time here is precious, every day. I teach others to not take for granted this time and space, and to not waste away your time here being asleep or walking through the motions.

This is one of my favorite chants, and it is best described through this passage:

I live in a house of miracles, held and guided by the light deep within me. Oh, so precious this lifetime I've been given, and I believe there's a magic that is about to begin, and I believe, I believe, I believe there's a magic. Ardas Bhaee, Ardas Bhaee Amar Das Guru, Amar Das Guru, Ardas Bhaee, Ram Das Guru, Ram Das Guru, Ram Das Guru, Sachee Sahee.

Letting go is part of life. Death is the only guarantee for each human, and so everyone must let someone else go. The seasons change, lives move on, the world is not the same. Our cultures do not stay stagnant, or return to any golden days of yore despite political pressure. You cannot return to any value fashioned out of old; nothing will ever be the same.

Life moves forwards, never back. We let go of each breath, each heartbeat. We let go of each birthday, each birth. We become very accomplished at letting go, and yet, it is so easy to fight nearly to the death to hold onto things. Letting go does not make us weak.

In fact, this is natural. We are eternal beings in bodies that die. This illusion of impermanence offends our endless nature to the very core. When we identify with the illusion, letting go wounds us. If we identify with our infinite nature, with the boundless creativity of the Universe, we begin to realize that letting go is a perfect part of constant expansion.

We can't think our way into this peace. We can't reason our way into this knowing. We must experience a connection with the larger plan to know this gentle grace. We must reach out to the Infinite and ask, "Are you sure?" in order for the Divine to lean down and whisper in our ears, "Yes!"

Choose the pain you need to let go of. Choose the fear, the anger, the thing you did years ago that you can't forget. Choose the situation you are ready to leave behind. And chant this mantra:

Ardas Bhaee, Amar Das Guru, Amar Das Guru, Ardas Bhaee. Ram Das Guru, Ram Das Guru,
Ram Das Guru Sachee Sahee.

-Spirit Voyage

This is a way of calling upon Guru Amar Das and Guru Ram Das (who represent the Hope of the Hopeless and the Lord of Miracles). It begins by affirming that what you are saying is a prayer. You then connect with their powerful energies. And then, with "sachee sahee," you release it and let it go. You know that your prayer is heard and it is done. This is the mantra of answered prayers, of moving beyond difficult situations, and gracefully letting go.

Need to "Let Go and Let God"? There's a mantra for that. And an answered prayer waiting for you just around the bend.

Guru Amar Das is the energy of grace and hope, when there is no hope.

Guru Ram Das is the energy of miracles, healings and blessings. This is the prayer to answer all prayers and one of my favorite chants. It is considered a mantra prayer, because it automatically combines the body, mind, and soul to align and integrate. And without saying what you want, your consciousness is adjusted all through your vibration and the energy it evokes inside your heart. It really encompasses how I feel about who I am and what I believe. My wish is that you, too, will see how precious your life is, that you too, will be guided by that light deep within yourself and that you, too will trust your inner knowing on your journey to yourself.

May the long-time sun shine upon you, all love surround you and the pure light within you guide your way on!
(Kundalini Yoga chant – Yogi Bhajan)

May you see all experiences as gifts for your growth, especially the ones that challenge you the most. When Renee lost her hearing, I learned to view challenges in this way.

Renee has been a real gift in my life, through the emotional and physical death she experienced in losing her hearing, to my going through my own death, as she went through her death of losing sound. This was a cathartic time in our lives. It was such a powerful journey, and one that I will never forget. I learned so much about communication and what it really means to communicate, not just with our words, but with our actions, energy, and heart. I think perhaps this is what woke me up to how I would choose to live my life. I remember, after she lost her hearing, taking her to a play group that we had participated in prior to the loss, and recognizing the sleep everyone else was in – and acknowledging how this tragedy woke me up.

I'm amazed at how much all of us take things for granted, how much we are not grateful for the everyday simple things, as well as the challenges in our lives. I never went back to that play group. I felt that none of the parents wanted to talk to me about my experience with Renee, and I was dying to voice what was going on, to be heard and to be held. We are not trained in how to hold space for one another. We are not trained in how to listen; we are trained in giving advice and following this low-self-esteem model of worrying about what we will say and how we will look. This is the illusion, because none of that really matters deep inside to any of us, and none of that encompasses who we really are.

Through the process of awakening all aspects of yourself, you begin to notice the parts that are asleep and hidden, and the parts that are alive. The feelings of aliveness grow, and begin to direct your life, in an abundant, miraculous way that creates even more juice and aliveness.

Being Alive in Life

> "Don't ask what the world needs. Ask what makes you come alive and go do it. Because what the world needs is people who have come alive." – Howard Thurman

We waste so much time doubting where we are going and not trusting our individual process. I invite you to begin to trust that what shows up is teaching you something. It is time to start being in the moment with yourself and each other, to take time for stillness every day. These are the qualities that will help you live your life to the fullest.

These are the qualities that will help you come alive. As Howard Thurman says, "Don't ask what the world needs. [instead] ask what makes you come alive [because that is] what the world needs…. How can you come alive? Where in your life are you not alive? There is so much magic to witness and be a part of – and this is what helps me to be alive.

I feel so empowered making conscious choices. I held to my vision of what I wanted for myself, my family and my own life. Trusting in my vision of what I desired is what directed my choices and the life I have created. To live fully in your heart, in reclaiming yourself over and over again, is to be alive.

To live an engaged life, one that is worth living, where no matter where you are or who you are with makes a life become magical and mysterious, and allows you to dance with it as it courses through you and directs you, is to be alive.

Now, after all these years, John and I are accepting of each other, by supporting each other through our friendship and our deep appreciation for how each of us has served the other's growth. The best part is that our kids get the best of both of us, the tools and consciousness of what I was asked to teach them as their mother, and the humor and grounding they received from their father. It was part of my journey to pass on these types of teachings to the next generation. It is part of my work here to support you in living a spirit-infused life, a life that offers you a connection to your own divine light and guidance, and offers you tools to tap into more of your joy and happiness. The truth of our time here is that we are here to grow into more love than we can imagine. We are here to learn to love ourselves more deeply – for in doing this, we love each other more deeply.

The result of all this wisdom I have gained is that we are here to forgive and touch the center of our hearts with each other. We are here to have a human experience in a spiritually infused life.

Soul Asks – How do you love me?

> Like the sparkle on the sea as the sun reflects off the turquoise blue.
> How bold you are and how willing to be in my depths. The balance of your shadow and your light and your ability to dance between the worlds of self and life.
> Through your commitment to me, your beloved and my creative expression through you.
> Your creative intelligence and ability to risk your ego to express your true self and love the depths of who you are.
> To express Love in all its forms and reflections and to follow your knowing, your inner guidance and to trust the light you hold within.

Do you have an interest in taking the next step on how to integrate the tools outlined in this book?

Would you like to embody a life of happiness from the inside out?

Explore the Be Whole Journey on my website at http://katiebsmith.com/ along with other options for coaching.

Designed to integrate your body, mind, and heart and access the wisdom they hold, the BE WHOLE JOURNEY supports you over a 12-month period, in living from a place where you learn to listen and trust yourself more, build on your strengths and build commitment to being an active participant in creating the life and work you desire.

This extensive experience is broken down into specific experiential exercises and topics that are simple, yet intentional, to fully cultivate a more fulfilling experience of how you bring yourself to your life and work.

Quotations to Empower

"The Breath is the tender charge of God"
– Yogi Bhajan

"Our relationships are not separate from our spiritual evolution. Our relationships are our spiritual evolution. Your relationships have become your temples! Do you love enough to allow for the possibility of perfection in whatever life shows to you?"
-Gregg Braden

"Everything you want is on the other side of fear."
– Jack Canfield

"It takes courage to grow up and become who you really are."
-e. e. cummings

"Those who don't believe in magic will never find it."
– Ronald Dahl

Our relationships perfectly reflect our own inner process; they are wonderfully effective mirrors to help us see what exists in our own growth. So, if relationship difficulties persist, it is a message to us that a deeper level of our own healing is needed.
– Shakti Gawain

"The practice of mindfulness is learning how to live your life deeply so you don't waste your life."
– Thich Nhat Hanh

"What you resist, persists."
– C.G. Jung

"The highest spiritual practice is self-observation without judgment."
– Swami Kripalu

"Commitment is what transforms a promise into a reality."
-Abraham Lincoln

"Acknowledgement is the only way to keep love alive."
-Barry Long

"Emancipate yourselves from mental slavery, none but ourselves can free our mind."
– Bob Marley

"You will never find peace of mind until you listen to your heart."
-George Michael

"Guilt is anger directed at ourselves- for what we did or did not do."
– Peter McWilliams

"Forgiveness is the final form of love."
– Reinhold Neibuhr

"We can only heal at the level of consciousness of which we are aware."
- Rochelle Schieck

"A Mantra is nothing more than a collection of words strung together to create a positive effect."
– Robins S. Sharma

"Life isn't about finding yourself; it is about creating yourself."
– George Bernard Shaw

"Progress is impossible without change, and those who cannot change their minds cannot change anything."
-George Bernard Shaw

"The secret to change is to focus all your energy, not on fighting the old, but on building the new."
– Socrates

"Don't ask what the world needs. Ask what makes you come alive and go do it. Because what the world needs is people who have come alive."
- Howard Thurman

"The most visible creators I know of
Are those artists whose medium is life itself.
The ones who express the inexpressible-
Without brush, hammer, clay or guitar.
They neither paint or sculpt – their medium is being.
Whatever their presence touches has increased life,
They see and don't have to draw.
They are the artists of being alive."
-Unknown

"Please think about your legacy, because you are writing it every day.
-Gary Vaynerchuck

"We don't simply fall into situations accidentally, but create them around ourselves based on our beliefs about reality. If we closely examine aspects of ourselves that are unsatisfactory, we can see that each uncomfortable or unworkable situation serves to show us our own misconceptions and mistaken attitudes. Once we have seen these for what they are, we can correct them or let them go."
– Gerd Ziegler

About the Author

Katie B. Smith

As an Executive & Career Coach, Katie B. Smith works with senior executives, managers, and professionals who want to:

1. Become more productive in their current role.
2. Develop into more inspiring leaders.
3. Improve their work satisfaction by aligning their work more closely with their values.
4. Seek new career opportunities.

Katie holds her Advanced Corporate Coaching certification from Coach U, a Professional Coach Certification (PCC) through the International Coach Federation (ICF), and is also a skilled Mentor Coach for coaches who want to increase their coaching skills and build their businesses.

A former Executive Recruiter, Katie spent over 15 years consulting and training professionals how to hire and retain top talent, and providing strategic consulting to increase profitability, reduce costs, build teams, increase accountability, and increase employee morale. Katie also holds the distinction of having coached C-Suite leaders in Fortune 500 companies.

Katie was chosen as one of the top 25 Career Coaches by Career Toolkit in 2016. Her many years spent helping companies find top executives as an Executive Search consultant gives Katie an inside perspective on what companies are looking for when they hire. She uses this expertise to support her Career Exploration and Job Search Coaching clients to successfully present their best selves to key companies, stand out in the crowd, and land the job of their dreams.

In addition to individual Coaching, Katie does Peer Group Coaching to support leadership development and team building. One group commented that they were wondering if Katie had put "truth serum" in the water they were drinking, because her insightful questions and supportive presence created space for them to speak truths that had festered underneath the surface for many years.

In 1990, Katie shifted her focus inward with a desire to redefine "success" in light of personal challenges, including raising a severely hearing-impaired daughter. While teaching her daughter to speak and to listen, Katie learned what it means to truly communicate. During this time, Katie discovered the power of yoga and meditation to reduce stress and increase creative thinking and communication.

This led to her building a much-needed stress management course for attorneys in the early 90s. She now presents various stress management and culture thriving topics nationally to corporations and individuals, bringing awareness to the importance of achieving an integrated, balanced life that allows participants to do their best work.

How to Work with Katie

Katie can help you uncover the crucial patterns, beliefs, and strengths that you need to navigate your path to success and **BE HAPPY NOW.**

Katie believes that seeking to uncover and to align with our authentic selves is vital to our becoming the best leaders we can be. Her clients often comment on her unique ability to help them identify tangible goals with personal and professional meaning, allowing them to experience more freedom, higher income, greater business results, and greater peace of mind.

Be Authentic – Awakening awareness in how you lead and work. These programs are for executives and leaders who want to improve their Emotional Intelligence, leadership competencies, communication skills and career navigation within or outside an organization.

Be Intuitive – Business owners interested in strengthening the qualities outlined in the Be Authentic program learn to build and to grow their confidence and trust in relationship to how they grow their business. This includes career professionals interested in being an active participant in creating their next career move.

Be Whole Journey – A 12-month experiential program that guides you in making sustainable change from the inside out. Includes a copy of Katie's book and Playbook Guide with weekly exercises. This includes 1:1 coaching with Katie and two experiential offsite retreats to support the integration of work practices on a deeper level.

Mentor Coaching – Coaches who are interested in getting their coaching certification and growing their coaching business and skills will benefit.

Peer Group Coaching – (Company sponsored program)

 Peer Group Coaching fuels professional and personal growth by bringing together small groups (6-8) of like-minded individuals at the same level of success. Peer Group Coaching combines the power of coaching conversations with the gift of peer support. Experience tremendous insights that can be quickly integrated and practiced. With the support of your Peer Group, you move beyond roadblocks that previously kept you stuck, to catapulting forward toward your goals. Peer group coaching supports the creation of collaborative cultures inside organizations, building trust, accountability and strengthening leadership competencies.

Mastermind Groups – Groups of individuals interested in working together to create forward movement in what they are creating, and moving towards their business and career goals as a group will find like-minded support.

Katie@KatieBSmith.com
http://KatieBSmith.com

 KatieBSmithExecutiveCoach   @KatieBSmith  KatieBSmith

Clients' Thoughts

Katie has the unique ability to help her clients connect and find their brilliance within. What's so interesting to me is that she does this by serving as a role model for her clients by accessing her own brilliance, and infusing that into her coaching sessions. Through coaching with Katie, I have been able to shift and open many doors that have been blocked. I've found a deeper sense of peace, confidence, and freedom in my life.

As I look back over my initial coaching prep sheets, I'm surprised at how those early goals have long become a way of life for me. And concepts that took longer to grasp like "You create your life," which I just could not understand for the longest time, have finally become a part of my understanding and propel me forward... to create my life. LOL!

Katie's wisdom is powerful. She has an unbelievable ability to listen deeply and hear what's being said – in words, as well as what's being said in the breath between words. Sometimes she will ask a question, other times offer thoughts... but I am always amazed at the profoundness of what she is saying as it relates to me at that moment. And I'm always amazed at the impact it has on opening my mind and heart to new understandings about myself and my world.

What I have loved the most, and which I believe has been so helpful to me in expanding my awareness and quality of life, are the simple yet significant things she has taught me. One of my favorites is learning that when I am sitting at my laptop with teeth clenched, hunched over working to meet a deadline or create something that is amazing, and nothing is working, that I need to leave my desk and shift up my energy. When I first started working with her on this, she said, "Just get up, go take a walk, give yourself some room." And I said "That's ridiculous... how is it going to help me meet my deadline by taking a break? That's going to make me a nervous wreck, because I will feel I need to be at my desk getting that work done." In another conversation on this same topic, she was able to help me understand that when I notice that my teeth are clenched or I'm hunched over, that my body is telling me I'm working in a place of fear. And fear cuts off all creative juices and actually makes things harder to get done. So, if I would just give myself permission to just this one time, give up the grip and walk away for a minute, I would be able to come back and get my work done with minimal effort.

I finally started to see the light and decided to give it a try. And you guessed it – it worked like magic. What's funny is that this has become such a natural part of my life... when I notice that I'm blocked, or my teeth are clenched, or my body is tense, I just naturally take a walk or go do something else to shift my energy. And when I come back to my work... it is always easy and better. In fact, I can't *not* work this way anymore.

Another thing that Katie taught me, which is small but has huge impact, is the power of our breath. I don't know about you, but I'd never given breathing a second thought. It just happens... thank heavens. But it turns out that breathing is my most effective tool at increasing mindfulness, and decreasing fear and anxiety. Who knew?

Katie coached me on this for quite some time... again, before I could get it. But now I think of my breath as my always on and always available best friend. No matter where I am, I have learned how to use my breath to get centered, calm down, enjoy the moment in a more delicious way, honor and acknowledge the moments of my life – good and not so good – and experience deep gratitude for my aliveness.

A forever life-changing tool, available all the time at no cost. All because of Katie. How cool is that! – Debbie Josendale, Small-Business Owner, Denver, CO

Katie was my executive coach as well as conducting group coaching for six manager-level employees. It was a challenging and yet rewarding experience for everyone. Katie is very effective at stopping the "story" and empowering individuals to take ownership and create life experiences that YOU want, rather than being a victim of circumstances. It's a bit challenging at first to go within oneself, but it's also incredibly empowering and freeing to let go of the external focus and rather only focus on oneself and how I want life to be, how I choose to respond to circumstances around me, etc. I could visibly see the transition of my staff as they evolved through the challenging aspects and came out the other side as much happier individuals as well as more effective managers. I highly recommend Katie individually as well as for teams.
– Beth Crump, Director of Clinical Global Affairs, Lakewood, CO

I've explored coaching before; now I am a believer. If you have a circumstance, opportunity, or obstacle you want to face head on, bring Katie along for the ride. Katie has proven her value over and over as a coach with relentless focus and impact. Embrace the change you know you need. It is real with Katie. – Caroline Wyatt, Vice President of Human Resources, Spokane, WA

Working with Katie has been a game-changing experience for both my current professional growth and future career

exploration. Her focus on expanding and leveraging my strengths, identifying opportunity areas, and understanding what my career outlook could be in the future has been eye opening. If you are looking to improve your professional skill set or seeking a coach for identifying other career opportunities, I recommend Katie to help with clearing this path.
– Erick Whittier, Business Team Leader, Denver, CO

A Reformed "Coach-Skeptic," that's what I would call myself. I now regularly recommend Katie B. to friends and colleagues. Katie's professionalism and leadership, and her intelligence and resources, have allowed me to take my professional career to new heights. Her intuition and EQ have also provided steady guidance – critical in navigating new professional and personal waters. I will continue to recommend Katie to friends and colleagues, and I am thrilled that she made an enthusiastic believer out of me! – Julie Huls, CEO, Austin, TX

As the CEO of a business, I've found that working with Katie has been invaluable in helping me stay accountable in my role as a leader and in growing the company. Katie's coaching has helped me better identify my blind spots, and hold me accountable to execute on strategies that improve my overall performance and therefore my organization. Katie has also helped my team strengthen our communication skills, and increase respect for our individual differences while providing new tools that allow us to work together more effectively. – Stephanie Klein, CEO, Denver, CO

Katie is a talented executive coach with a keen sense for enabling self-discovery, professional (and personal) growth, and recognizing your own potential. She does this by offering a unique viewpoint into how you think and perceive yourself and others. The result is the realization of new skills, and knowledge of how to capitalize on your strengths and use these tools to become a successful and authentic leader. I highly recommend Katie for those who are looking to develop their professional skills and relationships or are searching for greater focus and satisfaction in their personal and professional lives. – Tim Bauer, Director, Denver, CO

For the past year, Katie has been a mentor, coach and guide as I've navigated through tremendous personal and professional transition. We may not realize that we have the courage to live the life we want to live – however, with a bit of guidance, we're able to more clearly identify and hold onto our professional values, align them to our personal values and ultimately live the life we've intended for ourselves and our families. My professional life has taken many twists and turns during our first year working together. After fourteen highly successful years at a large global organization I'm on to a new, unforeseen journey, a path that I wouldn't have seen had I not developed an appropriate level of self-awareness. Fear has been replaced by excitement and empowerment. Katie has encouraged me to "flex" newly developed muscles, continue creating and ultimately, remain true to myself – easier said than done! I can't thank or recommend Katie enough. I'll make the same recommendation that was made to me over a year ago – get in touch with Katie! – Sean Lightner, Vice President of Sales and Marketing, Harrisburg, PA

I had the honor of working with Executive Coach/Mentor Katie B. Smith over a six-month period. I must say it was life changing. Katie provided both technical and practical advice. She listens intently & guides her client with a gentle but candid manner down the road to success. She assisted me in creating a "tried & true" method of system and language skills of both strength and delivery. I have recommended her services to many and will continue to do so. With much gratitude – Annette Flowers, Account Executive, Lakewood, CO

I have been working with Katie for several months and it has made a huge impact on me both personally and professionally. I have a different outlook on my career and am able to deal with various work situations more thoughtfully. As a result, I find myself more relaxed and less stressed, which has given me more energy. – Debbie Little, Assistant Director of Human Resources, Denver, CO

I engaged with Katie during a time of personal and career transition. The work we did together made me understand what I really wanted, and how to take steps and actions to not settle for mediocrity. I was able to direct my career aspirations that set me on a path to accomplish my short-term and long-term goals. Due to Katie's work, I truly feel that I can affect my future and have a road map to personal and career happiness. – Jason Winston, Director of Marketing, Denver, CO

I have worked with Katie off and on over the past couple of years, and I very much value her ability to gently yet effectively guide me in creating awareness, holding the intention of what I want, and acting on my intuition. Katie's balanced approach to career and life coaching helped me create a quality of life that benefits both me personally and my work. – Lindsay Faussone, Vice President of Business Development, Denver, CO

Katie has helped guide me through some big career transitions, and each time, I have ended up in a better place – both personally and financially. She has helped me develop strategies to make my life easier, and yet more productive. Katie is unique – a highly savvy business professional, as well as an intuitive counselor. The combination has been a powerful asset for me. If you want to make the most of your life, you will love working with her! – Theresa Casey, VP Business Development, Denver, CO

Katie Smith is an incredible professional coach. I hired her when contemplating starting my own business, and she has been an invaluable partner along the way. Katie's coaching approach in working through decisions brings out the best in an individual and gives confidence in the result. As a part of the coaching, Katie is constantly supplementing the sessions with additional resources that are very beneficial.

While this is my first time working with a professional coach, I would recommend it for anyone who strives to challenge yourself personally and professionally to become a better you, and I would recommend that Katie Smith is the partner to help you get there. – Eric Roark, CFO, Los Angeles, CA

I asked Katie to help me find the clarity I needed to truly know what it was I was meant to do and wanted to do next... and that's exactly what she did. Through her guidance and carefully crafted coaching, Katie helped me gain clarity at a time when things were incredibly cloudy in my career. After just a few sessions, I was able to see again and with that vision, I found what I was looking for... all of this within a two-month process. I couldn't be happier, and I know I have Katie to thank for getting me going! – Jackie Denier, Director of Studio Operations, Los Angeles, CA

Katie Smith has been an amazing resource with profound insight and very logical guidance. During a time of transition, she brings a sense of stability, providing a forward vision that is so needed. This neutral view of my career has been a huge benefit as I merge the past with the future direction while utilizing all the talents and skills I've developed over time. I find her bright, positive and uniquely able to tell me what is needed, just when it's needed. Finally, it is simply fun working with Katie. – Susan Musgrave, Business Development Director, Albuquerque, NM

I highly recommend coaching with Katie to others who want to increase their emotional intelligence at the workplace, and feel more comfortable about navigating the job market, developing a unique professional value proposition, and clarify/track professional goals. Katie helps the individuals she coaches by establishing clear goals and objectives for the duration of the engagement, and working toward those goals. Through my work with Katie, I learned how to look at the workplace differently, and to approach it with more confidence, and this work helped me in all aspects of my life." – Mark Sugarman, Vice President of Product Development, Los Angeles, CA

"Katie B. Smith is simply a great coach. I have had the privilege of working with her over a period of time and she has always been a powerful support in helping me move forward and achieve results. She is smart, intuitive and possesses a strong background of life experience that is valuable to me in my coaching relationship with her. I would recommend Katie to anyone who is serious about clarifying and moving towards their goals and objectives." – HB, Small-Business Owner, New York, NY

"Katie has many gifts that she delivers as you work with her through the coaching process. The biggest benefits that I received in working together were:

1. She seeks to understand you and what is holding you back from getting what you deserve. She digs in deep with you and uncovers areas of your business life and uses that to assist you in getting where you need to go.

2. She is high in EQ, and very positive always. She uses techniques to work with you as fast or slow as you need to progress towards your goal. She uses a variety of ideas, methods, and processes, which feels comfortable, because she is allowing you the time to understand and absorb these ideas at your own pace. When you work with her, it's not about being the same, it's about growth and getting to open up for more greatness in your life.
3. She is all about being your champion and helping you to secure what you want in order to be successful in feeling great about your desired path."

– Elaine DiLisio, President, Denver, CO

Katie is a terrific career coach who is engaging and helpful. She listens closely and also gets to the point to ensure your time together is effective. I enjoyed my conversations with her and always took away specific action items that were right for me. I highly recommend working with Katie to get really targeted in finding a job you'll love. – Sara Travison, SR. Business Analyst/ Product Manager, Long Beach, CA

"I highly recommend coaching with Katie to others who want to increase their emotional intelligence at the workplace, and feel more comfortable about navigating the job market, developing a unique professional value proposition, and clarify/ track professional goals. Katie helps the individuals she coaches through the establishment of clear goals/objectives for the duration of the engagement and working to those goals. Through my work with Katie, I learned how to look at the workplace differently, and to approach it with more confidence, and this work helped me in all aspects of my life." – Michael Schwarz, Vice President, Denver, CO

"I sought Katie's coaching services because I knew I wanted to experience growth both personally and professionally. I have learned so much through working with Katie; most importantly, how to take care of myself to improve my quality of life while still growing our company. I have become a much more effective communicator, both as a doctor and an employer. I highly recommend Katie as I feel each coaching session builds new awareness, improved strategies, and assists in creating a clear vision for growth." – Leah Hahn, D.C., Golden, CO

BIBLIOGRAPHY

Andrews, Lynn V. *The Power Deck, Cards of Wisdom.* New York, NY: HarperCollins, 1991.

Amundson, Ron. Kendrick Frazier, ed. *The Hundredth Monkey Phenomenon,* 1985. https://en.wikipedia.org/wiki/hundredth_monkey_effect

Braden, Gregg. *Walking Between the Worlds: The Science of Compassion.* Radio Book Store Press, 1997.

Bridges, William. *Transitions: Making Sense of Life's Changes,* 2nd ed. Cambridge, MA: Da Capo Press, 2004.

Dreamer, Oriah Mountain. *The Invitation.* New York, New York: Harper Collins, San Francisco, 1999.

Gawain, Shakti. *Creative Visualization, Use the Power of Your Imagination to Create What You Want in Your Life.* Novato, CA: Nataraj Publishing, 2002.

Goleman, Daniel. *Emotional Intelligence.* New York, New York: Bantam Dell, Division of Random House, Inc., 2006.

Iyengar, B.K.S. *The Tree of Yoga.* Boston, MA: Shambala Publications, Inc., 1988.

Jarrett, Christian. *"Gratitude: How Expressing Gratitude Might Change Your Brain."* New York, New York: *New York Magazine* blog, January 7, 2016. http://nymag.com/

scienceofus/2016/01/how-expressing gratitude-change-your-brain.html

Kaur, Guru Rattan. *Transitions to a Heart-Centered World*. Sanbury, PA: Yoga Technology LLC, 2014.

Kaur, Ramdesh. *Mantra for Letting Go: Ardas Bhaee*. Spirit Voyage Blog, November 4, 2010. http://www.spirit voyage.com/blog/index.php/mantra-forletting-go-ardas-bhaee/

Kaur, Sat Dharma, *"Yogi Bhajan on Forgiveness,"* April 8, 2016. http://beyondaddiction.ca/2016/04/08/yogi-bhajan-on-forgiveness/

Kundalini Yoga Research Institute. *Praaana, Praanee, Praanayam*. Espanola, New Mexico: Kundalini Research Institute, 2006.

Myss, Caroline, Advanced Energy Anatomy: The Science of Co-Creation and Your Power of Choice. Boulder, Colorado: Sounds True, audio book.

Schieck, Rochelle, *Qoya: A Compass for Navigating an Embodied Life that is Wise, Wild and Free*. United States. Inspire and Move Press. 2016.

The Coach U Personal and Corporate Coach Training Handbook. *"Removing Barriers: Identifying And Eliminating Tolerations"* Hoboken, NJ: John Wiley & Sons, Inc., 2005.

Wilber, Ken. "About the Author". https://integrallife.com/author/ken-wilber/

Ziegler, Gerd Tarot, *Mirror of the Soul*. York Beach, Maine: Samuel Weiser, Inc. 1988.

www.ingramcontent.com/pod-product-compliance
Lightning Source LLC
Chambersburg PA
CBHW070112080526
44586CB00013B/1270